It can be said ... formed by ma... ... ... intellectual knowledge in the world avails nothing if he is not guided and molded by the Holy Spirit. Paul has that intrinsic trait of molding knowledge and life experience that uniquely prepared him to write this book on miracles.

—JOHN RUPPERT
PHYSICIST, NASA JOHNSON SPACE CENTER

Paul Risser is a great storyteller. His skill in relating stories in a warm and congenial manner not only engages his listeners, but more important acts as a matrix to introduce spiritual truths. These stories of real-life experiences will have relevance that provide insight to the people who read the book.

—DAVID GULINO
EXECUTIVE AND CHURCH LEADER

To so many persons of all ages, Dr. Paul Risser is friend, mentor, pastor. His unforgettable sermons, always grounded in the truths of Scripture, are brought to life by his riveting and often humorous gift of storytelling, a gift that is now transferred into this book on miracles.

—DR. MARY ANN LIND
PROFESSOR, SPEAKER, AND AUTHOR

Dr. Paul Risser is truly an authentic man with outstanding leadership skills that have been forged through the fire that comes with ministry. Paul, who has preached all over the world, relates messages that exhibit incredible spiritual depth that only come as a result of walking the road of life. Humor, transparency, and unpretentious-ness yield powerful and captivating messages. You will see in this book on miracles his love for relating the experiences of people whose stories would not otherwise be told, or even noticed.

—Dr. Bill Kirkwood
psychologist

As a physician, I daily encounter people who come to see me whose problems are more spiritual than physical. I tell them they need a pastor more than they need a doctor. To my family and community of friends he is a great man but comes as a *servant* of the Lord.

—Dr. Ragaa Iskarous
medical doctor

"God is always finding ways to reveal Himself to us" was a theme that was constantly taught in our home. This book will help you capture the miracles He has custom-made for you.

—Pastor Terry Risser
Son of Dr. Paul Risser and
Sr. pastor of Florence Avenue
Foursquare Church

AN EYE FOR FOR MIRACLES

AN EYE FOR MIRACLES

DR. PAUL RISSER

Foursquare Media

AN EYE FOR MIRACLES by Dr. Paul Risser
Published by Foursquare Media
1910 W. Sunset Blvd., Suite 200
Los Angeles, California 90026

This book is produced and distributed by Creation House, a part of Strang Communications, www.strangbookgroup.com.

Unless otherwise noted, all Scripture quotations are from the Holy Bible, New International Version of the Bible. Copyright © 1973, 1978, 1984, International Bible Society. Used by permission.

Scripture quotations marked THE MESSAGE are from *The Message: The Bible in Contemporary English*, copyright © 1993, 1994, 1995, 1996, 2000, 2001, 2002. Used by permission of NavPress Publishing Group.

Scripture quotations marked NKJV are from the New King James Version of the Bible. Copyright © 1979, 1980, 1982 by Thomas Nelson, Inc., publishers. Used by permission.

Scripture quotations marked NLT are from the Holy Bible, New Living Translation, copyright © 2007. Used by permission of Tyndale House Publishers, Inc., Wheaton, IL 60189. All rights reserved.

Scripture quotations marked TLB are from The Living Bible. Copyright © 1971. Used by permission of Tyndale House Publishers, Inc., Wheaton, IL 60189. All rights reserved.

Scripture quotations marked KJV are from the King James Version of the Bible.

Design director: Bill Johnson
Cover design by Justin Evans

Library of Congress Control Number: 2010927641
International Standard Book Number: 978-1-61638-191-2

10 11 12 13 14 — 9 8 7 6 5 4 3 2
Printed in the United States of America

CONTENTS

Foreword

THE NEAR CENTURY-LONG STORY of the Foursquare Church is one that is filled with miracles. It's as true today as it was during its birth through the ministry of evangelist Aimee Semple McPherson. My friend, Paul Risser, a former president of the Foursquare movement, has recorded for us a number of these manifest evidences of God's power and grace of recent years.

Paul has written them not as a testimony to history but as an encouragement to the sustaining of our continuing *present* expectation, both today and among those of the rising generation. This book will speak to you, to say, "What is past is prologue to the future; what is written here is a prophecy of things that are to come." This expectancy finds solidity on the foundation of God's Word and will find currency wherever hearts remain faithful to Jesus Christ and available to His Spirit.

After I began my own term as president of the Foursquare movement following Paul's season of service in that office, our conversation one day occasioned his referencing a number of miracle stories he had heard in his own travels globally. I encouraged him to write this book, knowing he felt a sense of mission to relay the testimonies here. Now with the book's appearance, it is heartwarming to see the release of these pages—pages that will both profit and stimulate your faith.

Paul's travels with his wife, Marilee, both during his pastoral years in Santa Fe Springs, California, and as president, brought him into dozens of nations. There he ministered to missionaries and national leaders who serve as Foursquare Church missionaries and leaders of the scores of indigenous national movements related to this movement. They continue to multiply—a multiplication that stands as a testimony to the power of the Holy Spirit magnifying Christ as Savior, Healer, Baptizer with the Holy Spirit, and Soon-coming King.

At the time of this book's release, a typical year will find upwards of 2,000,000 souls coming to Christ annually, being reached through the more than 64,000 churches in 140 nations. May it be a resource serving at many dimensions—prompting passionate prayer and the pursuit of our praying and proclaiming God's Word with the expectation of a healthy proliferation of supernatural signs and wonders. With this, our greatest joy is to celebrate with heaven's angels the greatest miracle of all, the salvation of eternal souls, as God's mighty workings advance His kingdom of love and grace.

—Jack W. Hayford
Founding Pastor, The Church On The Way
Chancellor, The King's College & Seminary
Los Angeles, California

PREFACE

A Brief Personal Glimpse

My oldest son, Brad, was leaving home for West Point, and I had no doubts at all about the decision. I knew it was good and right and that Marilee and I had processed it with him every step of the way. This was a huge forward step in our son's life, and we were proud of and happy for him.

So where did all those tears come from?

Because I had to fly to the East Coast myself the day before Brad was scheduled to leave, I asked him to drive me to the airport. Normally our conversation would flow smooth and easy, but on that day it was hard for either of us to speak. I made several attempts to encourage him but soon realized I was really only talking to myself.

We parted with tears, and I immediately approached the ticket counter to change my seat assignment. Because I was a premier flyer with that airline, I asked for—and received—a window seat in the back of the plane with no one else in my aisle. Why? Because I needed to face the window when I cried and didn't want anyone to see me. When a flight attendant on board asked me if I was all right, I waved her off. I'd be fine. Just one of those pesky asthma attacks.

Why was I grieving? Why did I feel such desolation in my heart? It wasn't because Brad was leaving home to become a cadet. And it wasn't because I knew it would be a tough year for him, stretching him farther than he'd ever been stretched before. Those were all *good* things, positive developments in the life of my firstborn. I really couldn't have asked for a better set of opportunities for him.

What hurt my heart the most that morning was the overwhelming conviction that my influence in Brad's life was at an end. We had raised him, and now he was leaving home. Our opportunity to shape his life was history.

Or so I imagined.

Candidly, that has to be one of the most erroneous thoughts ever to enter my mind. I couldn't have been more wrong. The truth is, our years of influence as parents had just begun! Brad is now fifty years old, and in the intervening years since his graduation I have had more wide open doors to impact his life—and he mine—than we could have ever imagined. No, it would never be quite the same as when he lived at home, but the opportunities for input would be every bit as significant, every bit as profound, and every bit as satisfying.

Influencing the generations that follow us, I believe, is an innate, God-given desire.

I'm reminded of Moses as his earthbound life drew to a close and the words he spoke to those who would follow after him.

> But watch out! Be very careful never to forget what you have seen God doing for you. May his miracles have a deep and permanent effect upon your lives! Tell your children and your grandchildren about the glorious miracles he did.
>
> —DEUTERONOMY 4:9, TLB

In the course of pastoring two churches for thirty-six years, serving as the president of my denomination, and traveling to over one hundred countries of the world, I have some knowledge and some experiences I shouldn't be keeping to myself.

There are true miracles—the "glorious miracles" that have had "a deep and permanent effect" upon my life—that need to be declared, not for my honor or recognition but for His.

So you might say I wrote this book first with the Risser, Bigg, and well-connected Bird families in mind. Since my brother's passing, I am now the lone patriarch of the Risser tribe, and it falls on me to tell my children and grandchildren, nephews and nieces about a God who time after time breaks through natural law and human expectations to do that which only He can do.

Again and again, I have seen Him accomplish the humanly impossible and the wildly improbable, bringing healing and help and provision and great joy to me and to others who have been close to us through the years.

The reality is that someday, sooner or later, I'll be moving on to my true home in heaven, and from there on I really won't be able to influence my family anymore. At least not in a direct way, in person. But in the pages of this book, perhaps, they'll be reminded of what Paul Risser believed and experienced—and they, in turn, will pass those stories of His grace and power on to their children as well.

It's also important to me to write to the good people of the two churches in Texas and Southern California I pastored for more than three and one-half decades. I think particularly of the young people who grew up during my pastorates and became like spiritual children to me. I have a responsibility to declare God's mighty works to them, too.

Most of the miraculous happenings I describe in this book didn't occur in the bright radiance of a spotlight, on a platform surrounded by a sea of people, or under the glare of TV lights. What follows in these pages are stories of real people who found themselves painted into impossible corners; cried out to God; and found deliverance, provision, protection, strength, and wisdom beyond any reasonable expectation or natural explanation. Most of these miracles occurred in "the course of life":

◆ A medical doctor's "chance" encounter in an upscale department store with a woman in great physical danger

◆ A sudden compulsion to visit a young mother—at the very moment she plans her suicide

◆ A mysterious pickup and driver on a remote road in Trinidad, rescuing a preacher from a deadly ambush up ahead

◆ An atheistic, communist Chinese professor unexpectedly leading an up-and-coming government official to the very feet of Jesus

◆ A brilliant brain surgeon experiencing a meltdown when he encounters God's love

One last thought. When Jesus performed miracles, signs, and wonders in the pages of the Gospels, it not only ignited faith in the hearts of the individuals to whom He ministered; but, it also changed the lives of those who watched it unfold before their eyes. Men and women who desperately needed their own touch from God suddenly found the faith and courage to stretch out believing hands toward heaven. A testimony has a powerful effect on someone in need of a miracle.

It's my prayer that this book will move you, the reader, to believe God for what you have never dared to believe Him before.

Miracles will result from that belief for the simple reason that what God has done for others, He can certainly do for you.

Acknowledgments

- Marilee, my wife, who has been my greatest encouragement in every aspect of my life.

- Those who began encouraging me to write a book for which I had no interest: Pastor Randy Remington, Allen Quain, and Carol Ann Shima.

- Dr. Jack Hayford, who made it possible to turn a spiral notebook into a book; connected me with Larry Libby, an exceptional editor; and provided this book for pastors.

- Don Pickerill, professor and pastor, who helped me avoid any theological pitfalls.

- People who gave input and information: Leslie Glassford; Ellen Hagemeyer; Dr. Leland Edwards; Mary, the ninety-eight-year-old wife of Harold Williams; missionary Lewis Ziegler; Dr. Don McGregor; Dr. Dick Scott; and Dr. Ron Williams.

INTRODUCTION

An Eye for Miracles

God can do anything, you know—far more than
you could ever imagine or guess or request in
your wildest dreams! He does it not by pushing us
around but by working within us, his Spirit deeply
and gently within us.

—EPHESIANS 3:20, THE MESSAGE

I N THIS DECLARATION WE hear that God is not only able
and willing to do anything that we could possibly asked
for, but that He is even willing to go beyond the bounds of our
prayers.

Many consider this to be one of the highest and greatest
doxologies in all of Scripture. The apostle Paul, highly educated
as he may have been, seems to be groping for superlatives that
might somehow come close to describing God's greatness,
majesty, and magnificence. We can almost feel his frustration
with his inability to describe the indescribable, explain the inex-
plicable, and to measure the immeasurable.

After observing miracles through all the years of my life, I
have come to a few conclusions about these supernatural intru-
sions into the ordinary course of a day's events.

First, every miracle has an *element of surprise* attached to it.
Second, every miracle is marked by the fragrance of something
completely fresh and new. You never get accustomed to God's

interventions in daily circumstances. Third, *a miracle cries out to be recognized*, giving our loving, faithful Lord the recognition and praise He deserves.

To accomplish these things, I believe we need to allow God to gift us with something that will set us apart and elevate our hearts for the rest of our days. I call it an eye for miracles.

A Change in Perspective

I can't tell you the exact day or hour when I began to see things differently. I suppose you could say the realization has come upon me slowly.

I remember returning to my hotel room in San Antonio brimming over with excitement after a long morning stroll along that city's famous River Walk. If the walk itself took me two hours, it probably took every bit of an additional hour for me to describe everything I had seen to Marilee.

No doubt about it, I was as proud as could be over my captured images of south Texas charm. It had been a perfect morning for picture taking, with seemingly endless inviting and artistic camera angles. Magnificent clouds. Quaint Spanish architecture and lush landscaping. Sunlight sparkling off the river. Venerable oak trees. Shadows on staircases. Perfect petals on tiny flowers. And shadows, old houses, sunrays, ivy, arches, faces, doors, children, fountains, bridges, cafes, shops, rows of pottery, and on and on.

Anticipating another such experience the following day, I hit the streets once again. But somehow, the magic was gone. I walked along the same picturesque streets at the same time of day, seeing many of the same sights, and nothing seemed to move me at all. I came back after thirty minutes complaining about the miserable, muggy weather and feeling totally uninspired.

What made the difference in those two adventures on subsequent days? Just this: On the second day, I left my camera in the room.

Could that really be true? Could a seemingly small matter like carrying a camera actually make such an outsized difference in my perceptions? I decided to test my theory by going out again that very afternoon—this time, with my camera in hand. I'm sure it must have been even hotter and muggier than it had been earlier in the day. Flies may have buzzed around my head, rude tourists may have jostled me, and obnoxious music may have assaulted my ears. But to tell you the truth, I didn't notice any such thing. San Antonio had blossomed for me all over again. How could one city be so laden with allurements? I couldn't get over how lovely that winding river walk looked in the long rays of the late afternoon sun. I stayed out for an hour and a half and came back in awe.

All of this has been something of a revelation for me. As an amateur photographer, I have, over time, trained myself to see potential pictures everywhere. At first it was mostly snapping pictures of my young sons when they were doing something cute or amusing, but my interest grew exponentially from there. As it did, I began to realize how much more beauty and wonder I was encountering in life. Just by having my camera with me— and even without snapping pictures—I found myself more apt to see things along the way that I would have otherwise missed: landscapes, cloud formations, sunsets, engaging angles, and intertwining lights and shadows, not to mention countless potential close-ups.

My conclusion? Having (and carrying) a camera has helped me develop an eye for beauty beyond any inclination I had ever possessed before. Bottom line: I see life differently. I truly believe I experience my waking moments at a different level—a higher level—than before, when I seemed to have very little peripheral vision at all.

That's just the way it is for people who have cultivated a photographer's eye. Two people with identical 20–20 vision can walk the same distance along the same forest path at the same hour of the day and report vastly different recollections of the experience. Ask the first person, "What did you see?" and he or she might tell you, "Well, I saw a trail and trees—oh, and some rocks, too. Really nothing much." Ask the next person and you might get a reply more like this: "I saw dew drops glistening on tiny flowers in the moss. I noticed how the sun shone through the spring maple leaves, making them seem translucent. I watched the pattern of shadows play across a rock wall. I spotted a hawk perched on the top limb of an old, dead tree protruding from a crag."

So here's my question: What would it be like if we applied this same principle to our relationship with God? How would life be different if we developed *an eye for miracles*, His supernatural fingerprints on our daily, workaday world?

EYES OF THE HEART

The apostle Paul must have had something like that in mind when he prayed for his friends in Ephesus, "I keep asking that the God of our Lord Jesus Christ, the glorious Father, may give you the Spirit of wisdom and revelation, so that you may know him better. I pray also that the eyes of your heart may be enlightened in order that you may know the hope to which he has called you, the riches of his glorious inheritance in the saints, and his incomparably great power for us who believe" (Eph. 1:17–19).

You've heard of how teachers (and mothers) are said to have eyes in the back of their head. But did you know that all of us who belong to Jesus Christ have been granted *eyes of the heart*? That means the ability to see what would otherwise be invisible: the supernatural acts and gifts of the loving God who constantly involves Himself in our world and in our lives.

In the Book of Genesis, we read about an "eyes of the heart" moment in the life of young Jacob as he was fleeing to Aram to escape the vengeful anger of his brother, Esau. The Bible says that he left Beersheba and set out for Haran, and "when he reached a certain place, he stopped for the night because the sun had set" (Gen. 28:11).

In other words, he stopped when it got dark. As far as Jacob was concerned, this "certain place" was just a random piece of turf where he could lay down on the ground and get some sleep. And he wasn't too particular about accommodations! Scripture relates that "taking one of the stones there, he put it under his head and lay down to sleep" (Gen. 28:11). (Now that's a tired man!)

We might be tempted to say that any of us sleeping on the bare ground with a rock for a pillow would experience some troubled sleep or a few strange dreams. But what happened to Jacob that night in the middle of a land that would someday bear his new name—Israel—was more than a dream. It was an encounter with the living God. Call it a stairway to heaven, call it Jacob's ladder, call it anything you like; but when that young traveler woke up in the morning, he knew something mighty big had happened on that small, nondescript piece of Canaan where he had lain down.

The Bible describes it like this:

> When Jacob awoke from his sleep, he thought, "Surely the LORD is in this place, and I was not aware of it." He was afraid and said, "How awesome is this place! This is none other than the house of God; this is the gate of heaven."
>
> —GENESIS 28:16–17

Jacob memorialized that place, giving it a name, *Bethel*, or "house of God." That was probably a wise thing to do—and certainly an understandable response to what he had just experienced. But there was nothing really special about Bethel as a place. He might have walked five more miles down the road that night before he laid down, and then that place would have been called Bethel. The real significance of that night was that this young man had a very personal encounter with God. As a result, the God of his father and grandfather became *his* God.

"Surely the LORD is in this place, and I was not aware of it!"

The Message translation renders Jacob's words in Genesis 28:16–17 like this: "GOD is in this place—truly. And I didn't even know it!...Incredible. Wonderful. Holy. This is God's House. This is the Gate of Heaven."

Have you ever found yourself saying words like that? The fact is, you could make the exact same statement about where you are right now, at this very moment. Whether you know it or not, whether you've thought about it or not, whether you are aware of it or not, God is in that place.

What place? *Any* place.

Your favorite overstuffed chair in the family room. Seat 12D on the 737 headed from Seattle to L.A. Your bed. A little table at your local Starbucks. A lawn chair in your sunny backyard.

He is there. And He leaves His remembrances, love notes, fingerprints, and calling cards in the most unexpected places. You must have eyes of the heart to see them. My prayer is that our good and gracious Lord Jesus who loves you so much will use this book to bring light, clarity, and fresh focus to the spiritual sight He has already given you.

When that happens, it won't only bring benefit your life, it will touch the lives of all who come in contact with you. Let me illustrate.

EYE OF THE BEHOLDER

My missionary friend Ron Williams and I walked together on a soft, humid evening in Hong Kong, one of my favorite cites in all the world. I knew it would be a remarkable time because I had my camera with me!

Nearing the world-famous Aberdeen Harbor, we looked out across a lovely stretch of water crisscrossed by sampans and junks. On our way to the water's edge, I noticed several older Chinese women sitting in the unique, dignified way that they do and conversing with each other. I was struck by their faces, so weathered, wrinkled, and kindly.

I thought they were beautiful.

At my prompting, Ron spoke to them in Cantonese. He told them we thought they were beautiful ladies and wondered if we might photograph them. The women gave their approval by sitting up even straighter and gracing us with radiant smiles.

As I knelt down to shoot some close-ups, a group of American teens sauntered by. One of the boys piped up and said, "What do those guys see in those old women to take so many pictures?" A couple of them laughed, and they walked on by.

Some time later, Ron and I had turned back, retracing our steps to the car. The Chinese ladies were still there, but this time they were surrounded by those same American young people we had encountered earlier. All of them had their cameras out, not only taking pictures of the ladies but posing with them—laughing and having a high old time.

I know enough about travel, photography, and human nature to understand that none of these young people would have ever looked twice at those lovely women if they hadn't seen us taking their pictures. But after noticing us paying attention to the ladies, it must have registered with them that they might be missing something pretty special after all.

I've seen that happen again and again. Start taking pictures of something, and some people get curious. They'll stop to see what you're photographing and will find themselves taking an interest in things they otherwise would have never noticed at all.

These simple stories are the best way I know how to express the purpose of this book. When, as a little boy, I not only saw but experienced multiple miracles in the life of our family, it was as if God had given me a divine camera. The eyes of my heart became enlightened, and from that time forward I have seen miracle after miracle.

Yes, there are those who would say that what I've seen and experienced weren't miracles at all but random happenings or coincidences. It was that way in Jesus' day, and it will be that way until He returns. Some see the fingerprints of God on the events of their lives, and others don't see Him at all. Some, with Jacob, will look around in amazement at their surroundings and say, "Surely the LORD is in this place, and I was not aware of it . . . How awesome is this place!" Some will rub the sleep out of their eyes in the morning and see *Bethel*, the very house of God. Others will see only see a primitive camping spot, a few square yards of rocks and dirt; shrug their shoulders; and go on their way.

CHAPTER 1

THE MIRACLE THAT
GOT MY ATTENTION

I'M SURE I WAS no older than a second grader when I observed a miracle at our house that stuck with me for life. It was a significant event, giving me an extra sensitivity to recognize miracles. I do not want to be perceived as a little spiritual prodigy. I was, in fact, just a typical kid who loved the things every other kid enjoys: playing with toys, playing sports, and enjoying the good things of life. But I also remember being fascinated with people, especially the ones who came to our house.

Our house and church in my childhood were like Grand Central Station. Because my parents had a gift of hospitality, we had people coming and going all of the time. We hosted denominational leaders, pastors, missionaries, nation-changers, and even people like R. G. LeTourneau, the most noted Christian businessman of his day. To me they were *all* extraordinary people, and I would dash home to try to get them to come out and play ball with me or go to the creek and swim in our dammed-up swimming hole.

I remember this particular incident as well as if it happened last Sunday night. My dad and mom loved missions, so they frequently had missionary services. On one particular Sunday we were privileged to have the missionary statesman Dr. Harold

Chalfant. I can't remember what his official office was at the time, but consistent with his values, he lived and breathed missions. My memories of childhood and youth categorize Dr. Chalfant as one of the greatest preachers on Earth.

That Sunday night Dr. Chalfant took the audience on an imaginary journey on the back of a water buffalo through the insufferable heat of a swamp, surrounded by deadly predators waiting to eat us if the buffalo made a misstep. We were on our way to a savage tribe in the "green hell" jungle of Bolivia. Missionaries had lived in the jungle for years and had introduced the natives to the Lord and a new and blessed life. Dr. Chalfant's imaginary journey predated television, but his descriptions were clearer than anything you would see on a screen. He had every little kid on the edge of their seats. I couldn't imagine why anyone would go to those dangerous places.

Chalfant urged, "In our effort to the reach the world with the gospel, some are called to *go,* and others are called to *give.*" After the sermon he gave opportunity for people to give, most sacrificially. The majority understood they couldn't go, so they gave. Later, when our family arrived home, it became obvious to me some had overdone their giving.

There was a dynamic that had taken place during that offering. My mother and dad, sitting on the opposite sides of the church, each had a twenty-dollar bill. Mother and Dad had money in their savings, but those two twenty-dollar bills were to cover our weekly living expenses. They each knew the other had twenty dollars. When the offering plates were passed, my mother put her twenty dollars in the plate, assuming my dad would have kept his. Likewise, my dad put his twenty dollars in the plate, thinking my mother would have kept hers.

All was fine until we arrived home from church. My dad matter-of-factly asked my mother for her twenty dollars because he would need it the next morning. She told him she had given her twenty dollars in the missionary offering. My dad then told her that he had given his twenty dollars in the offering. The incident struck them so funny that they began to laugh to the point of tears from amusement. It didn't seem funny to me. At a time when they should be worried, they were acting as if this were a big joke, a time for hilarity. My thoughts were along a different line: "We are going to starve! The Risser family is broke! And my parents are laughing!"

My dad was nonchalant when he said, "Don't worry! The Lord will take care of us."

My mental response to that statement was, "That's their solution for everything!"

Because I am a student of the ways children process things with respect to their parents, I am aware that almost every kid, at some stage, arrives at the conclusion that his or her parents are weird. For most kids, this usually doesn't happen until adolescence. Well, I must have been mature for my age because that night, at the age of seven, the weirdness of my parents became a reality to me. It rattled me to realize that I was a member of such an abnormal family. My parents were odd. They were laughing when they should be crying. This was all strange to me. I had a hard time going to sleep that night.

I recall being contemplative at school all of the next day. At dinner that night at the end of the meal, everyone stayed at the table until we were dismissed, as was the custom at our house. Dad began reminding us of the previous night and how he had told us that God would take care of us. He pulled out a letter from our Uncle Paul in Los Angeles that had come in the mail that day. Uncle Paul had written something like, "Dear Otto and Martha, the Lord prompted me to send you a check because you have a financial need. So I enclose this check." We all took a turn looking at the check. When my turn came, my little mind went to work. It was for five hundred dollars! I didn't realize there was that much money in the whole world, and we only needed forty dollars! If that check was provided from the Lord, it was special to see that He gave way more than we needed.

My mind was churning. Uncle Paul would have had to send the letter several days earlier to get it there that Monday when we needed it. All of this registered in my little mind, and then I got it! They were laughing the night before because they must have known the money was going to come. At least that is how I processed it. Then I mused, "Maybe they're not as weird as I thought."

I think that experience became, as it were, my "camera" that gave me an extraordinary awareness of the supernatural workings of God.

WHAT IS A MIRACLE?

A few days ago I was having lunch with a successful young businessman. He did not question the reality of miracles and was interested that I was writing a book on miracles, but he asked a probing question: "How do you define a miracle?"

In response to that question, I refer to what I think is the best definition of a miracle, encapsulated in a biblical event recorded in Genesis 18:1–15. The story goes like this. God came to the home of Abraham and Sarah, bringing a couple of angels with Him. Abraham encouraged them to stay, washed their feet, and had them rest while he had a fine meal prepared for them, as any polite Bedouin would do.

While they were eating, they were making small talk. "By the way, where's your wife, Abraham?"

"Oh, over there in the tent," he answered.

Then the Lord nonchalantly tells Abraham why He really showed up. "In about a year Sarah will have a son."

Sarah must have had her ear to the tent door, because she heard that statement and began to laugh and mutter to herself. "Ha! That's ridiculous. How could a worn-out old woman like me enjoy such pleasure, especially when my husband is even older and more worn out than I am?"

The Lord had really good hearing, because He said to Abraham, "Why did Sarah laugh? Why did she say, 'Can an old woman like me have a baby?'"

It is doubtful that any of us would have a problem understanding Sarah's reasoning. Conventional wisdom, even back then, would tell us that you don't give birth to a baby when you are ninety years old and your husband is ninety-nine. She had been hoping for decades that she would have a child. God even kept promising them that they would have a son. Why would He wait until now? They had long passed the point of physical possibility. As far as Sarah was concerned, God had waited too long. Why didn't He come when they were in their thirties, or even their forties? I'm for Sarah. Why wouldn't she laugh?

I am not prepared to answer for God, but I have found a common thread throughout Scripture that carries on into twenty-first century life. God seems to *delight* in allowing situations to turn into impossibilities where there is no solution except for God Himself. When all sources of human remedy have been exhausted, He breaks onto the scene.

To me, the Lord's response to Sarah's stifled laugh and flawed reasoning is a key, if not *the* key, that leads to a good definition of miracles: "Is anything too hard for the LORD?" (Gen. 18:14). God asked that sticky, rhetorical question of Abraham and Sarah. It is sticky because it should stick in all of our hearts and minds to be asked every time we face an impossible situation. It is rhetorical because the answer is so obvious that it goes without saying. The conclusion is self-evident: "No! Of course not! Nothing is too hard for God." So a miracle is when something that was heretofore beyond human solution is manifested when God interjects Himself into the situation and brings a divine solution.

Jesus said reaffirmed the whole concept in Luke 18:27 when He declared, "The things that are impossible with men are possible with God" (NKJV).

- No sickness is too bad that God cannot heal it.
- No storm is so turbulent that He cannot calm it.
- No disappointment is so overwhelming that He cannot redeem it.
- No giant is so large that He cannot conquer him.
- No mountain is so big that He cannot bring it down.
- No financial crisis is so severe that He cannot remedy it.
- No relationship is so broken that He cannot mend it.

CHAPTER 2

THE SOUR EXPERIENCE THAT TURNED SWEET

J ACK PURTELL IS A dynamic man and an exceptional, optimistic farmer. He lived with an infectious excitement for the Christian life—and seemed constantly overwhelmed with the greatness of Christ.

Although he had been a believer for years, when he first started attending our church he was new to many aspects of the Spirit-filled life. Always an eager learner, he definitely wanted his life to be everything God intended!

Jack was one of the first people I ever had the privilege to pastor who truly had the gift of giving. He gave with reckless abandon. While some asked, "How much do I have to give?" his quest always seemed to be, "How much *can* I give? How far can I go?"

Whenever I think of Jack, I think of the phrase from the Psalms: "Delight yourself in the LORD" (Ps. 37:4). Jack did that, literally. He found pleasure in the Lord and sought to maintain his focus on God no matter how busy or hectic his life became.

It was so typical of him (but exciting nonetheless) that he would propose setting aside some of his best acres as a special gift toward a missions project, above and beyond his regular, generous giving. That was the arrangement: Whatever the yield might be, it would belong completely to the Lord.

What's more, Jack wanted our church council (all knowledgeable farmers) to pick those acres as we thought best. After a tour of his four cotton farms, we settled on what seemed to us to be the best of the land for the Lord's use that year.

Can you imagine how exciting this was for me as a young pastor? I knew in my heart that this was a test, like God mentions in the Book of Malachi.

> Bring the whole tithe into the storehouse, that there may be food in my house. Test me in this," says the LORD Almighty, "and see if I will not throw open the floodgates of heaven and pour out so much blessing that you will not have room enough for it."
>
> —MALACHI 3:10

In my heart I knew that God would pass this test with flying colors.

Back when I was in high school, our family went to Detroit to visit the Ford plant, and the first afternoon we went by the track where they were driving at high speeds, maybe thirty cars at a time.

Someone asked, "Is this the *test* track?"

"No," the Ford engineer answered, "this is the *proving* track."

It was more than semantics. Keeping their eyes on the ultimate objective, this was the track where they would prove that the cars were as good as they claimed to be.

To me, this matter of Jack Purtell's experience wasn't a test of God; rather, it was an opportunity for Him to prove Himself. And I felt absolutely sure that He would. He would show Jack and all the world what He could accomplish when people put

Him first. It was going to be a bumper crop, and as far as I was concerned, we could take it to the bank before the seed was ever sown.

But it didn't turn out the way I had expected it to. Not at all.

A few weeks into the project, I asked Jack how everything was going. He told me that for the first time in his years of farming his crops seemed overrun with insects. He had always been attentive to see there were adequate insecticides applied in the growing process, and this had always taken care of the situation. He had never needed to hire a plane to do crop-dusting.

Never, that is, until this year. And he was compelled to do it twice.

Weeks later, I built up my nerve to ask him again about the crops. "Well, Paul," he said, "this is the first year I can remember when my crop has been overtaken with weeds. I haven't done anything different, but this year there are weeds everywhere. We've had to do the weeding twice."

I must say that this was bothering me much more than Jack. He was spiritually grounded and an eternal optimist with respect to anything to do with the Lord, and he seemed confident that it "would all work out somehow."

But I had thought it was sure thing! I had thought it would be a slam-dunk for God!

I don't even want to comment on how disappointed I was with the Lord. As far as I remember, I never expressed my disillusionment out loud, but I do remember remonstrating with the Lord in private. "Lord, You only get so many opportunities like this, and for some reason You're letting it slip by! You have no idea how hard this is on me as the pastor. I've been telling these people about Your promises—'Give and it will be given to you…' Well, look how much Jack has given, and You've let him hang out to dry! This could have been such a teachable moment for the people, and now it looks like the opportunity will be wasted. Well Lord, I've learned one thing. I'll never get involved in something like this again!"

For all my complaining and handwringing, however, the situation only seemed to get worse rather than better. The next-to-last nail in the coffin was when Jack got a call from the cotton gin about the quality of his harvest. The gin informed him that his crop, which normally averaged two bales of cotton per acre, had been so sparse that it was now averaging only three-quarters of a bale per acre. It was the worst yield in Jack's whole career of farming.

As a pastor in that Texas community, I had schooled myself in farming, just to be able to relate to my congregation, who were mostly all, in one way or another, connected to agriculture.

Nevertheless, I knew that the Lord had one last opportunity to redeem this whole experience, and that would take place when they graded the crop. At harvest, there is a grading system that helps buyers determine the value of the cotton. There are two standards. One is the grade, and the other is the staple, which is the measurement of strength. If Jack's crop could receive good marks on its grade and staple, disaster might yet be averted.

But I was so nervous about the results that I really didn't want to see Jack for fear of hearing bad news.

In a town our size, however, it was inevitable that Jack and I would run into each other, and I would have to ask him about the final grade. I'm afraid I must have stammered and stuttered a bit as we talked. I didn't want to find myself apologizing for God, but I may have come close to it.

Jack, however, laughed out loud, and apologized for not contacting me sooner with the final report.

The terrible grade Jack's cotton received that year would have normally brought the very least amount of return in the world market. But this year, for some strange reason, the demand for lower grade, lower staple cotton had soared to its highest price ever. When all was said and done, Jack's accountant called and said, "Jack, do you realize that you made more money this year than you've ever made in your career?"

My reaction was, "How in the world could that happen?" But God's acres had done just fine that year in spite of my worries, agonies, and dreads. What a valuable lesson I learned in experience. Never finalize or pass judgment on an experience with God until it is totally completed, which may or may not be in this lifetime.

For weeks after that report from Jack, I quoted and preached the Lord's words from the Book of Isaiah: "'My thoughts are nothing like your thoughts,' says the LORD. 'And my ways are far beyond anything you could imagine. For just as the heavens are higher than the earth, so my ways are higher than your ways and my thoughts higher than your thoughts" (Isa. 55:8–9, NLT).

And after quoting the Scripture I would pray—sometimes right out loud—*"And thank You, Lord, for not letting me forget it!"*

CHAPTER 3

IN THE NICK OF TIME

G. CAMPBELL MORGAN, THE PASTOR of the London Westminster Chapel, was known for his great preaching. He once wrote:

> I am never tired of pointing out that the Greek phrase translated, "In the time of need," is a colloquialism, of which the "nick of time" is the exact equivalent: "That we may have grace to help in the nick of time. Grace just when and where I need it."
>
> I have noticed in almost every miracle, it is not only the supernatural action of God that is in play, but usually there is a timing factor that comes into the grand design. At times it is timing that becomes the heart of the miracle. God frequently does His greatest acts, just "in the nick of time."

ONE HUNDRED DOLLARS

When we were beginning our ministry, my wife and I attended our first pastors' convention in a big city.

After the last evening session of the conference, I got into my car to drive back to our room in the hotel. On the way, I saw a young couple walking together on a sidewalk.

A voice in my heart said, *Stop and give that couple a hundred dollars.*

My first response was annoyance. "Where did that came from? Was that from the Lord, or just me? Well, whoever you are, I'm not going to give anybody one hundred dollars."

I had been directed by the Lord to give money to people and causes scores of times. But I was certainly not stopping on the street and giving money to total strangers—who may or may not have been part of our convention.

"Ridiculous," I said to myself. "You can't just walk up to people you don't know and say, 'I need to give you a hundred dollars.'"

It's not that I didn't have the money. I had learned from my dad always to carry two fifty-dollar bills in my wallet in case of an emergency—but surely not to hand it willy-nilly to complete strangers! They would think I was some kind of crazy man.

As the years have gone by, I've learned to clearly discern the Lord's voice, distinguishing it from random thoughts or impulses. But at that time, I just wasn't sure. (Or at least *told* myself I wasn't sure. Deep down, I think I knew it was the Lord all along.)

That inner voice spoke to me again as I saw the couple, still walking together on the sidewalk, as I looked back in my rear-view mirror. *Stop and give that couple a hundred dollars.*

By that time, I knew very well what the Lord wanted me to do. But I still felt too embarrassed to do it.

I started negotiating with the Lord. I told Him I would drive to the end of the block and circle back. If the couple were still on the sidewalk, I would stop and give them the hundred dollars.

Even then, I cheated.

I kept driving beyond the end of the block. In fact, I drove quite a few more blocks before circling around and driving back. Surely the couple would have moved on by that time!

It was getting dark, and as I approached the place where they had been standing, I couldn't see anyone. They'd gone back! I couldn't give them the money, after all, I reasoned. But no; there they were, right where they'd been, holding hands and facing one another in intense conversation.

"Maybe I shouldn't disturb them. Maybe they would resent someone interrupting their private conversation."

I knew that argument was hollow even as it crossed my mind. I had to stop. I'd already told the Lord that I would.

Pulling the car over to the curb, I got out and walked over to them. I introduced myself, and they told me they knew me. They had been attending the convention, too. I told them I felt the Lord had directed me to give them one hundred dollars.

The wife broke into tears. She told me they were just starting out in the ministry, that this was their first convention, and that it had cost more than they had expected or planned on.

The tears became a flood. "We have to drive five hundred miles home tomorrow," she sobbed, "and we had no money for gas or food. We were just standing here praying and asking God to help us. And here you came."

I thought to myself, "I could have come ten minutes ago if I'd done what God had asked me to do."

Her husband began to weep, too. "You are a Godsend, Pastor Risser."

It was my turn to start crying. I was so glad they didn't know that I'd tried to get God to stop talking to me! We prayed and embraced and said our good-byes.

As I got back into the car, I felt so good that I wanted to yell out the window, "Does anyone else need a hundred dollars?"

A CALL FROM HEAVEN

After ten years pastoring my first church (in Brownfield, Texas) and after much prayer, deliberation, and quite a few tears, the day finally came to leave that church and accept a new pastorate.

The church to which we'd been called, the Florence Avenue Church in Santa Fe Springs, California, was about as different from our church in Brownfield as we could have imagined. Brownfield was an agricultural community of ten thousand in the wide open spaces of the Texas panhandle. Santa Fe Springs was very much a part of the Los Angeles environs with a population of over twelve million.

We loved our Brownfield church, and on the Sunday I announced our departure, I found myself full of sorrow. And wouldn't you know it! That Sunday the church was filled to capacity, the worship was especially joyous, and several people made decisions for Christ. After church, a number of people came up to us with tears in their eyes, asking us to reconsider and stay.

Spending time alone that afternoon, I began to question my decision, and the enemy filled my mind with doubts.

"Well, you've really done it this time, Risser. You're about to make the mistake of your life."

"You will regret this!"

"You'll never find a church as good as this one."

"Southern California? The big-city culture? You may have done all right in a small town, but you may fall on your face in Los Angeles. And once you go, that's it! You can never come back again."

I sat there in misery, at my wits end. My first inclination was to pick up the phone and call some of my friends to get their opinions. But deep down I knew that I needed divine confirmation. I went to my office, and in thirty minutes the phone rang.

Dr. Vincent Bird, one of our denomination's leaders, was on the line. He was also my brother's father-in-law and was like a relative to me. He and I had corresponded with each other by letter but had never talked by phone until that afternoon.

"Paul," he said, "I just want you to know that I visited Florence Avenue today. While I sat there in church, I thought to myself, 'Paul is going to do great here.' I just thought you should know that."

That word washed away my indecision and anxiety like a refreshing rain.

How could I ever doubt the miraculous timing and courage imparted by his affirmation?

SENT FROM L.A. TO N.Y. TO ANSWER A PRAYER

We were on our way to visit our son during his first year of college in New York.

When we arrived in New York City, we found ourselves behind schedule—and in a hurry. We had promised to be at a certain place at a certain time. Thankfully, we had set up the car rental in such a way that all I had to do was go in, give my signature, and drive away.

As I stepped up to the counter, however, the representative seemed excited to see my church's name on the paperwork. She looked me right in the eyes and said, "Do you know anything about Spirit-filled people?"

Uh-oh. I could see my wife in the waiting area out of the

corner of my eye, and I knew she was concerned about our arriving on schedule. Obviously, this was no time to get involved in a counseling session—or even a prolonged conversation. I wanted to smile and say, "I'm sorry, but I don't have time to talk right now. Converse with the next pastor who comes in. I'm in a hurry!"

But I didn't say that.

Instead, I rather jokingly replied, "Not only do I know about Spirit-filled people, I *am* one."

I asked the Lord to calm the agitation I was feeling. My parents had always taught me that interruptions are often God's opportunities.

The rental car representative told me she had been a Christian for five weeks. Just two weeks before, she had experienced the baptism with the Holy Spirit at a charismatic Catholic prayer meeting. Life had been really good since then, and she'd enjoyed five unbelievably happy weeks. Until just the day before. She admitted she had been bombarded by Satan, who was trying to make her doubt the reality of her recent experiences.

I quickly explained to her that this wasn't unusual at all. In fact, it's exactly how the enemy works. Though God won't give up on you, Satan will do anything to get those who are new to the faith to give up on God. This is Basic Satanic Strategy 101.

Her response surprised me. A huge smile crossed her face.

She went on to tell me that when she arrived at work that morning, she had been terribly depressed and wondered if what had happened to her over the last few weeks had even been real. Before her shift began, she went to the employee lounge, flopped down in a chair, and prayed, "Lord, if all of my experiences are real and from You, please send someone into the office to encourage me."

"And here you are," she beamed, "the answer to my prayer."

Since no one else was in my line, I took a moment to pray for her, asking the Lord to continue to strengthen her, encourage her, and protect her from every attack of the enemy. When I left, she was one happy lady.

Sometimes I try to see things from God's perspective. In this case God knew before either of us was born that this lady would be questioning her experiences with God and that she would pray and ask for encouragement. God decided to be creative (as always, He never does anything the same twice) and arranged to send me to New York and to that rental center to be an answer to her prayer.

"You know what?" I said. "You don't have to worry about a thing. The Lord will make up for the time I just spent with a hurting, doubting woman."

In case you're interested, we arrived at our destination fifteen minutes ahead of time.

GOD SAID, "I'VE GOT LOTS OF MONEY"

When we had our new sanctuary built, we ran into challenges not anticipated that set us over the budget by several million dollars. The monthly payment against the loan was almost scary. At the same time the economy of southern California went in reverse due to the huge loss of the aerospace industry. Many people from our church had to relocate to find jobs.

So, our reserves of $750,000, which had been set aside for emergency, were eroding at the rate of $15,000 to $20,000 each month. This went on for several months. I had no excuse for allowing myself to go into a state of discouragement, but it was keeping me from sleeping. During this time in my life I was so focused on our financial minefield that I dreamed in numbers. I calculated in my dreams how many years it would take to lose all our reserves and for us to go over the financial abyss. I was so sleep-deprived that I was going through life like a person just going through the motions.

At this point my encouragement was from my wife, the world's greatest optimist, and our business-astute church council, who gave me assurance there was no need to worry because soon the economy would turn around. Being with those men and women was alleviating my uneasiness.

But the crowning jewel came the next Sunday morning after the first service of the day. I was gathering my Bible and sermon notes to leave for my study. Out of the corner of my eye I noticed Percy Sickles coming up the steps.

Percy had a quiet and retiring personality, which overshadowed something you wouldn't surmise—he was a decorated hero in the Solomon Islands in the South Pacific during World War II. He was both a consummate warrior and a spiritual giant. He loved to pray and attended every prayer meeting that was called. But I hasten to say he never knew a thing about the financial business of the church.

When Percy came to the to the pulpit, where he had never been before, I could tell he was uneasy and felt he was overstepping his bounds. I tried to calm his apprehension by saying, "Percy, I'm so glad you came up to see me."

He got right to the point. "Pastor, while you were preaching the Lord talked to me about you."

I asked, "What did He tell you, Percy?"

He continued, "He told me, 'The pastor is worried and can't sleep and is on the verge of exhaustion. You need to talk to him.'"

Believe me, he had my attention, compelling me to ask, "What did He tell you to do?"

He answered, "He told me to tell you that you don't need to worry anymore about the church finances, because He has lots of money."

In a flash, it was as if the Lord had taken a huge load off my shoulders. I was so grateful to Percy, I wanted to hug him to pieces. And, I was so in awe of God that I wanted tell the world what He had just done.

Today, I am still impressed with the simplicity and straight-forwardness of Percy's interpretation of what God wanted him to tell me.

His words were like oil to my emotions.

Now, the proof is in the pudding. I have heard so many people who overuse the phrase, "The Lord told me," yet if you follow through their prophecies come to nothing. They are clouds without rain.

So, I was going to watch and test the fruit of Percy's prophecy. The first indication came the next month, when instead of coming short by $15,000 we went over the budget by $20,000. Before the economy returned we were always well over budget, no less than $12,000.

Let me make the point that there are millions of people who walk with the Lord and find the abovementioned experience not just to be a promise to a church but to us individually and to our families and businesses.

CHAPTER 4

AFRICAN DOLL

THIS IS A TESTIMONY I heard from Dorothy, a missionary nurse, who tells this story best in her own words:

One night I had worked hard to help a mother in the labor ward, but in spite of all we could do, she died, leaving us with a tiny, premature baby and a crying two-year-old daughter. We would have difficulty keeping the baby alive, as we had no incubator. (We had no electricity to run an incubator.)

We also had no special feeding facilities. Although we lived on the equator, nights were often chilly, with treacherous drafts. One student midwife went for the box we had for such babies and the cotton wool that the baby would be wrapped in.

Another went to stoke up the fire and fill a hot water bottle. She came back shortly in distress to tell me that in filling the bottle, it had burst. (Rubber perishes easily in tropical climates.) "And it is our last hot water bottle!" she exclaimed.

As in the West it is no good crying over spilled milk, so in Central Africa it might be considered no good crying over burst water bottles. They do not grow on trees, and there are no drugstores down forest pathways. "All right," I said, "put the baby as near the fire as you safely can, and sleep between the baby and the door to keep it free from drafts. Your job is to keep the baby warm!"

The following noon, as I did most days, I went to have prayer with any of the orphanage children who chose to gather with me. I gave the youngsters various suggestions of things to pray about. I told them about the tiny baby, explaining our problem about keeping the baby warm enough, mentioning the hot water bottle and that the baby could so easily die if it got chills. I also told them of the two-year-old sister, crying because her mother had died.

During prayer time, one ten-year-old girl, Ruth, prayed with the usual blunt conciseness of our African children. "Please, God," she prayed, "send us a hot water bottle today. It'll be no good tomorrow, God, as the baby will be dead. So please send it this afternoon."

While I gasped inwardly at the audacity of the prayer, she added, "And while You are about it, would You please send a dolly for the little girl so she'll know You really love her?"

As happened so often with children's prayers, I was put on the spot. Could I honestly say, "Amen," to such a bold petition? Frankly, I just didn't believe that God could do this. Oh, yes, I know that He can do everything; the Bible says so. But there are limits of what one can expect, aren't there? The only way God could answer this particular prayer would be by sending me a parcel from the homeland. Not very likely! I had been in Africa for almost four years at that time, and I had never, ever received a parcel from home. Anyway, if anyone did send me a parcel, who would put in a hot water bottle? I lived on the equator!

Halfway through the afternoon, while I was teaching in the nurses' training school, I received a message that a car had pulled up at my front door. By the time I reached home, the car had gone, but there on the veranda was a large, twenty-two–pound parcel.

With tears pricking my eyes, I felt I could not open the parcel alone. I sent for the orphanage children. Together we pulled off the string, carefully undoing each knot. We folded the paper, taking care not to tear it unduly. Excitement was mounting. Some thirty or forty pairs of eyes were focused on the large cardboard box.

From the top, I lifted out brightly colored, knitted jerseys. Eyes sparkled as I gave them out. Then there were the knitted bandages for the leprosy patients, and the children looked a little bored. Then came a box of mixed raisins and sultanas—that would make a batch of buns for the weekend.

Then, as I put my hand in again—could it really be?— I grasped the object and pulled it out. Yes, it was a brand new, rubber hot water bottle. I just sat there and wept.

I hadn't even asked God to send it; I had truly not believed that He would—or could.

Little Ruth was in the front row of the children. She rushed forward, crying out, "If God has sent the bottle, He must have sent the dolly, too!" Rummaging down to the bottom of the box, she pulled out the small, beautifully dressed dolly. Her eyes shone! She had never doubted!

Looking up at me, she asked, "Can I go over with you and give this dolly to that little girl so she'll know that Jesus really loves her?"

"Of course!" I replied.

That parcel had been on its way to our mission station for five whole months, packed up by my former Sunday school class, whose leader had heard and obeyed God's prompting to send a hot water bottle, even to the equator. And one of the girls had put in a dolly for an African child—*five months before*—in answer to the believing prayer of a ten-year-old to bring it "that afternoon."

Before they call, I will answer.

—ISAIAH 65:24

CHAPTER 5

PROBLEMS THAT REQUIRE SUPERNATURAL REMEDIES

ONE SUNDAY NIGHT, LONG after the church service had concluded, I was deep in conversation with Frank, a friend and church council member, when Ann Georgianna approached us. Since we could both see she was in distress, we immediately stopped our conversation to find out what might be troubling her.

Ann, at that time, was over seventy years old—a classy and beautiful lady who brimmed with charm. She was part of a large family, all committed Christians, that had emigrated from Sicily. When the parents of this family lost their health, it was Ann who offered to leave her vocation to care for them full-time with the generous support of her brothers and sister.

Under Ann's tender care, however, the parents lived much longer than anyone had expected. By the time they passed away, Ann was well past retirement age herself with virtually no Social Security benefits and precious little savings.

Making use of her gracious spirit and God-given charm, she found a new career as a hostess at one of the area's most popular restaurants—and quickly established herself both as a fixture and a favorite of the clientele. For several years, everything went well for her. She had her health and thoroughly enjoyed her role at the restaurant, which she proudly described as "the job the Lord gave me!"

That Sunday night, however, Frank and I could immediately see that something wasn't right with her. Her smile was gone, as was the usual sparkle in her eyes. And the first thing she said to us seemed so out of character for this gregarious, godly woman. "Pastor," she said, "my life is ruined! I don't know what to do. I'm *ruined*!"

"Ann," I said, "what has happened?"

She explained that the owner of the restaurant, with whom she related so well and who had always treated her with such favor, had hired a new general manager who decided to make wholesale changes.

"He told me he's going to *go young*," she said, which meant that a twenty-something, good-looking girl had already been hired to replace Ann, who was to be terminated in thirty days.

"You know, Pastor," she reminded me, "I have only a tiny bit of Social Security and just a little in savings, which would only take care of me for a few months. I'm worried sick. I know I can't get another job. Who would hire a lady my age? They want *youth*. I try to pray, but I think my prayers hit the ceiling and bounce down on me. Pastor, what shall I do?"

The grief was in her face, in her voice, in her eyes.

She was looking to me for answers, and at that moment, I didn't have a clue what to tell her. She had walked with the Lord so many years and had always been a strong believer in the faithfulness of God. What could I say to her that she didn't already know?

But she did know that I loved her. Frank and I stood with her that night, and she knew that we cared and that we would pray.

Sometimes I have found that people going through dark times gain more comfort when you quietly stand with them, acknowledging what they're going through and being strong for them "as in Christ's stead." If I'm a good pastor, I will put myself in the place of the one who is hurting. She didn't need a pastoral platitude; she needed to sense that I understood the gravity of her situation. I asked myself, "How would I feel if I were a seventy-year-old lady about to lose my job, with almost no retirement to carry me through? I think I would be a bit panicky, too!" Those sorts of thoughts kept me from offering up some worthless cliché in that moment, like "Keep looking up!" or "Don't worry when you can pray." Little solace there!

Many times as a pastor I found myself tempted to try to figure out natural solutions to problems with supernatural proportions. In Ann's case, for instance, one of my first thoughts was, "Maybe some of the wealthier families in the church would be willing to take turns supporting her."

But that wasn't the solution, and Ann would have never accepted it.

What Ann needed was a miracle.

A miracle takes place when God steps into our circumstances with divine wisdom, riches, and power to provide a solution from other than natural means. I've always had plenty of good ideas for God about how to resolve a variety of intractable problems, but I must admit that He has never used one of my suggestions. Instead, He uses a divine solution no one would ever think of.

Perhaps our best mental process is to rid ourselves of all our human answers and pray the prayer of Jehoshaphat, king of Judah, when the nation found itself in a catastrophic predicament. That godly king prayed, "O our God…We do not know what to do, but our eyes are upon you" (2 Chron. 20:12).

With hands on Ann's shoulders, Frank and I began to pray out loud for her. We reminded ourselves that it is in the time of weakness we are made strong and that God's glory shines the brightest in the darkest times. We submitted Ann's problem, which to us seemed impossible, into the hands of an almighty God, to whom the solution is very possible. We asked Him to lift this heavy load from Ann's heart and give her a peace and quietness. We told the Lord that we would no longer consider this Ann's battle or our battle any longer but that it belonged to Him. We ended our prayer by asking the Lord to not only solve this dilemma but to give Ann a huge victory in the process.

Ann tried, but even then it was difficult for her to keep her head up. We let her know that we understood her emotions, and if we were in her place we would feel the same way.

Ann went back to work on Monday, and the new manager seemed to gloat as he assigned her menial tasks that she would be expected to do during the final month of employment. She would say later it was one of the most belittling experiences of her life and that "things couldn't get any lower." The manager had a real cruel streak and laughed at her distress. Ann wondered if she had grace and strength enough to last through those final four weeks. As we talked on the phone that first Monday evening, Ann said, "Pastor, I'm about to break."

I felt so inadequate but made what attempt I could to help her refocus on the presence and faithfulness of God. "Ann," I said, "you've walked with the Lord longer than me, and you have told me some wonderful stories of God's faithfulness. You *know* He can be trusted. He will guard you against being tested beyond your capacity. He will lift you out of this very soon. The walk through the fiery furnace is brief, and you will come out unsinged. Let's believe together that this trial is almost over."

Ann was in no mood to share my optimism. "I'm counting on you to be strong for me, Pastor. Pray for me!"

As it turned out, the Lord didn't keep Ann waiting for her answer very long. On Wednesday of that week, I received another call from Ann—and it was about as different from the Monday call as two conversations could be. I could tell her spirits were sky high as she literally yelled into the phone, "Pastor! *A miracle has taken place!*"

Giving me no more than a couple of seconds to absorb that news, she quickly went on to explain. "Pastor, the owner of the restaurant came in today and *fired* the new manager—and told him to take the 'new girl' with him. He came into the back room where I was doing the humbling work and said, 'Ann, go home and put on one of your nice dresses and return to your position as hostess. I'm going to give you a good raise in salary.' Pastor, can you believe it?

"Pastor, it's God!" she said in awed tones. "It's *God!*"

But that was just the beginning of Ann's saga, as it swept over her life in joyous, recurring waves. God had the last laugh when, at the end of the month, in a restaurant with scores of employees, Ann was chosen as Employee of the Month. It was the very month the new manager had told her would be her last.

After another month, she had a conversation with a middle-aged couple who were regulars at the restaurant. To Ann, this husband and wife showed no signs of affluence. To the contrary, they looked and dressed so plainly she at times thought to herself, "How do they afford eating here two or three nights a week?"

She was surprised when they stayed until all diners left, evidently wanting to speak to her. Then they quietly asked Ann if she would come and work with them. They admitted they had been watching her for a couple years and had concluded she was just the person they were looking for. Whatever her salary might be, they said, they would *double* it.

Taken aback, Ann asked them, "What kind of business do you have, and what would you want me to do?"

They confided that they were building a privately owned country club in the foothills of the San Gabriel Mountains, including a huge golf facility and a large, first-rate restaurant with a spectacular view overlooking the valley. They wanted her to be their hostess, and even though the facility wouldn't be complete for nine months, they would give her that time off to herself, with pay.

"You'll be your own boss, answerable only to us."

It certainly seemed like the miracle she wanted, but was it too good to be true? As so many of us do, she began looking immediately for the barriers that would keep it from happening.

"San Dimas? I couldn't drive back and forth from where I now live," she said. "It would be much too far." They answered that they were building a large, opulent home with a guest house, which would be hers to live in.

Ann found yet another barrier. "But my old car is worn out, and I would need to make weekly trips to my church and to my family."

Ann couldn't believe their response. "We will buy you a car!" (It turned out to be a Cadillac.)

What was left but for her to graciously accept God's miracle provision for her life?

In the course of time, she invited my wife, Marilee, and me to visit her in her new living quarters, see her car, and have dinner in the beautiful dining hall overlooking the valley. On numerous occasions Ann said to us, "God is so good to me that I have to pinch myself to see whether or not this is all real."

For several years Ann was the much-loved and endearing hostess of the country club dining room, lived in the guest quarters of the palatial home, and lived in a state of awe over the extravagance of God's blessings. (I should also note that she frequently invited us to her club to have dinner and play golf.)

One day an investor came to offer the owner of the country club a handsome price he could not refuse. The sale was negotiated. But what would happen to Ann? She didn't have to worry about it for a moment. One of the only stipulations made in the contract was that Ann would be kept as a public relations employee as long as she desired to work there and would receive regular increases in salary. She continued on with her hostess responsibilities for several more years until age began to take its toll.

She finally quit working and went to live the last three years of her life with her "world's best brother," finally taking her leave to be with the Lord when she was ninety-three.

It comforted me—and made me smile—to realize that those successive waves of miracles would continue in the life of Ann Georgianna for all eternity.

CHAPTER 6

A DIVINE BLANKET

I DON'T KNOW WHAT IT was that inspired Mary Westberg to write to me on Christmas Day, 2003, but opening her letter a few days later was like a late Christmas present. Many of us in our denomination remember and honor her long years of evangelistic and pastoral ministry alongside her husband, Wayne.

Not many people know it, but Mary was the human vehicle the Lord used to lead the noted Lutheran author, pastor, and teacher Larry Christenson into his experience with the Holy Spirit. He, in turn, led a great Charismatic renewal among Lutherans specifically and also among many other traditional and mainline churches.

In her letter, Mary reminded me that she was now ninety-two and spent much of her time reflecting with great joy on the long years of ministry she had enjoyed with her husband. The intent of her letter was to remind me and anyone else who read her words of the greatness and kindness of the Lord.

Since it was Christmas, and cold, she related an experience from one of the first churches they pastored back in the Midwest. They had arrived at their new pastorate in the dead of winter and the freezing cold. The church was so new that there was no parsonage yet, just some crude living quarters in the back of the drafty church building. Difficult as it may be to believe, there was no heat in the building and no insulation.

Somehow, possibly not even knowing when their new pastor would arrive, the little congregation had neglected to provide a way for them to stay warm through a freezing winter night.

Mary, however, exuded the attitude so characteristic of her generation, who lived through some terribly difficult times but constantly rejoiced over God's faithfulness. She recalled that first night in particular, when she and Wayne were so cold they actually worried about their survival. Huddled together in the dark little church, they had two thin blankets, with newspaper packed between them, and wondered how they would make it through the night. As with so many pioneers of the faith, Mary turned to prayer before any other option.

She wrote, "I decided to pray, saying, 'Lord, please give us a divine blanket. We know You can provide that for us. Give us a divine blanket.'"

And just that quickly, they were strangely warm.

Her husband turned to her in the darkness and asked, "Honey, where did you get the blanket?" She wondered if he would even believe her when she replied, "It's a divine blanket."

Whatever it was, it kept them through that bitterly cold night. She added, "Isn't that just like the Lord?"

On subsequent nights, the little congregation (no doubt chagrined over their lapse) brought piles of blankets and heaters, but on one of the worst nights of their lives, Wayne and Mary had the Lord to protect them and cover them.

CHAPTER 7

NOT ONLY A GOD OF AMERICA

G EORGE PATSAOURAS IS ONE of my dearest friends, for whom I have a special love. Dr. Edwards, our missions director, gave me permission in 1976 to recommend that George, who at that time was a young lawyer, be appointed as the pastor of our denomination's only church in Greece at that time and also name him as the national director of that country. (Today that little church of twenty has grown to over fifteen hundred members.) I have followed George's ministry for years with great interest and delight. He has served a country where, up until just recently, every obstacle was placed against the way of the advancement of a non-Orthodox church. Praise the Lord that barrier has been lifted.

☙

George was the young pastor of the Foursquare church in Athens, Greece, meeting on the fourth floor of a rented facility only about three blocks from the Acropolis. Though the congregation was very small and poor at that time, George had prophetic visions of what the Lord expected them to be: "a church to the nations."

Fervently believing that prophecy and call, the believers there sought to poise themselves for growth. In fact, the rented hall in which they met was so large that the tiny congregation almost got lost in its immensity. They agreed in prayer in the midst of a cavernous space.

George, however, realized that once people did start coming, there wouldn't be chairs to accommodate them. With this in mind, the young pastor wrote to his friends and fellow pastors in the U.S. to ask for a special donation: Would they be willing to help the Athens church buy chairs to accommodate their anticipated growth?

The mailing turned out to be a costly affair—expensive in both time and production costs. On the very day when George was on his way to the post office to send the letters on their way, however, the Lord unexpectedly spoke to his heart.

Stop. Don't send these letters.

Obedient to that directive—but greatly puzzled—George walked back to the car with the unmailed letters. It was then that the Lord spoke to him in a more straightforward way: *Why are you writing all the way to America to ask money for your Greek church? Am I an American God, or am I a God to the entire world? Am I so inadequate that I can't provide the money for your Greek congregation without seeking funds from the Americans?* The Lord impressed upon George that He could provide from that congregation.

George quickly perceived that this would be a turning point both for himself, personally, and for the little church in Athens.

And so it was.

THE CHALLENGE

In a few days, George told his congregation what the Lord had said to him as he was about to mail those fundraising letters. He reminded the people that God was the God of the Greeks as well as the Americans and that He wanted to work through them.

That sent a buzz through the congregation. It excited them to think that God wanted to work through them and that they didn't have to rely on foreign help. And just as George had perceived, the moment became a turning point for the Athens church.

George went on to challenge each individual and family to total the number of people for whom they were praying to come to their church and then to purchase the requisite number of chairs to accommodate those people. In a short time, the meeting hall began to fill up with new chairs. And then it began to fill up with people to sit in those chairs.

George, too, began to purchase chairs. In his mind's eye, he could see the auditorium filling up with Greeks and then people from all over the region, so that the church in Athens would truly become a church to the nations.

And that is just what happened.

People began filling the auditorium, mostly Greeks at first, but then immigrants from other nations—from Russia, Iraq, Iran, Bulgaria, Albania, Turkey, Egypt, Poland, Romania, Spain, Morocco, Cyprus, Crete, Sri Lanka, and lands even beyond these. As a result, the church began to translate their services into numerous languages.

PACKED TIGHT

I visited their church in that location on various occasions.

From the pulpit, you could look to your left through a huge window and see the ancient Acropolis, where the apostle Paul himself had preached in Acts 17.

On the Sunday of my visit, the auditorium was crammed

with people. Regular attendees had prearranged to give up their chairs when newcomers came into the hall.

Quoting Psalm 37:23, which says the steps of a righteous man are ordered of the Lord, George Mueller observed that the same Lord also ordered the *stops* of a righteous man—the steps and the stops.

The Lord stopped George Patsaouras on the way to the mailbox with an appeal to American donors, and to this day George and his wife, Margarita, look back on that aborted trip as one of the most powerful things to happen to their Athens church. When the tiny congregation of Greek nationals grappled with the truth that God could provide for His work as effectively through the Greek people as through Americans, it broke a spirit of poverty that had kept a grip on their church and its members.

After that, there was no looking back. The fourth-floor meeting hall that had once seemed so large and cavernous became much too small for the multi-ethnic crowds desiring to squeeze into the auditorium. Everyone realized the church would have to find a larger facility.

So it was that the little church that a few years earlier couldn't afford chairs bought a prime downtown Athens property to build their own seven-story, multi-million–dollar facility. (No matter where you are in the world, it's invariably true that a church with a big vision will attract people with substantial financial resources.)

George and Margarita now pastor the largest evangelical church in that nation, ministering to the highest and lowest levels of Greek society. The church also houses a theological training center in which many of the immigrants are being trained to go back to their home countries in Eastern Europe and the Middle East to plant churches.

After this Athens congregation learned the miracle of God's provision, they went from being a receiving church to a giving church, investing in kingdom work all over the world.

CHAPTER 8

THE ROAD TO RUIN?

A T ITS GENESIS, THIS book was intended as something of a family chronicle. It was my hope to speak through these pages to succeeding generations of the Risser, Bigg, and Bird families, reminding us all of the greatness and faithfulness of God. The following story is intended for my boy, the one who actually traveled the road to Texas with us, before the younger two were born there. This is pure Risser lore, but of course you're all invited along for the ride.

ᘓ

I didn't want to be a pastor.

What's more, my wife didn't want to *marry* a pastor.

I remember assuring her (with laughter) that if she married me she would be safe from that fear. Although we both had good role model pastor fathers, we didn't feel we were cut out for such a calling. We were going to live happily ever after, involved in vocations we both enjoyed. We would pay our tithes, give to missions, and be faithful church members. And why in the world wouldn't the Lord be satisfied with that?

I was so sure that pastoring wasn't in my future that I even served for a time as a youth minister at the church pastored by my brother-in-law, Warren Twyford. He kept telling me he was grooming me for the pastorate, but it didn't worry me much. I knew better. Warren and I had been close, and he was always my biggest supporter. Ultimately, however, I knew I'd have to disappoint him.

Little did Marilee know that out of her hearing her father, a district overseer of churches, was encouraging me to pastor a church in Texas! One time I told her, "I wish you'd tell your dad to leave me alone, because I'm not about to take a church. That's the last thing I will do."

Nevertheless, he kept quietly urging me to reconsider, chipping away at my resolve.

Finally, although there were no bells, whistles, or audible voices from heaven, I surprised myself by succumbing to Dr. Bigg's constant prodding.

As a result, Marilee had to face her boss and explain our seemingly off the wall decision to go into the ministry. The senior vice president of the company she worked for was appalled.

"It's a waste of your lives," he told her. "If you want to help people, why don't you both join the Peace Corps and get that out of your system once and for all."

On my side of things, I had to sit down with the owner of the company where I worked. He was a thoughtful and caring individual who had shown me exceptional favor and was grooming me for a larger role. He had promised that if I would stay with the company for the long haul, he would quickly move me up the ladder. I could count on growing responsibilities and steady financial gains.

After I explained my decision to become a pastor, he blindsided me with the worst question possible.

"How much money are you going to make?"

I was sorely tempted to exaggerate at that point but instead told him the unvarnished truth.

"Fifty dollars per week," I said.

I wasn't prepared for his reaction, to say the least. His face grew red, and he paced around the room in agitation. I fully realized that to a man like him what I was doing was the most foolish thing in the world. Slumping back down into his chair, he bent forward with his head between his knees, like he was going to be sick.

When he raised up again he had fire in his eyes.

"You are doing the worst thing a parent can do!" he said. "You're depriving your children of their education. Listen, Paul, you're getting ready to go down the road of financial ruin, from which you will never recover. Think about it! Think what you're doing to yourself. Think what you're doing to your beautiful wife, to your son, and to the children that will come. *You will never be able to educate your children.*"

Under normal circumstances, I'm by nature an optimistic guy, never prone to discouragement, depression, or allowing circumstances in my life to eat me alive. (That didn't happen until later, after I had committed myself to the ministry!)

The CEO's grim assessment that afternoon, however, went like a dagger into my heart. I couldn't get those words out of my mind. "You are on the road to financial ruin, from which you will never recover."

As time went on, I abbreviated that prophecy to, "You are on the road to ruin."

Foolishly, I let this dismal prediction sink into my mind-set. I reasoned that while we still had the money I would buy a couple new suits, assuming these would be the last new suits I would ever be able to buy. We also went out and bought a new Volkswagen bug on the assumption this would most likely be our last new car ever.

As Marilee and I traveled along the interstate highways from California through Arizona and New Mexico, I found myself wondering if this was really the road to ruin. Had the Lord meant to use the gloomy words of our superiors to deter us from a disastrous path? Had I plowed straight through a red light? Was God trying to stop us before we drove off the edge of the earth?

Something in my heart refused to believe such a thing. And before we reached the border of Texas, I determined to get a grip and have a little talk with myself. "This is not the road to ruin," I told myself. "This is the road to *Texas*. We are in the Lord's will, and we're on a blessed and exciting journey."

As the miles went by, Marilee and I discussed the measures we could take to assure us of God's financial favor on our lives. She took notes as we talked.

First, we would commit ourselves to be good stewards of the money we would receive, whatever the amount.

Second, as both our dads had advised us, we determined to invest our savings and live strictly off of our income. The fact is, God can bless and multiply our income, and doesn't need our savings to provide for us.

Third, because we wanted and needed God's exceptional blessings on our lives, we committed to *doubling our tithe* to the Lord's work. We had both grown up seeing this principle exemplified in our homes: If you are in a financial bind, you shouldn't consider pulling back on your tithe, but you might consider doubling it. As the Lord says in the Book of Malachi: "Bring all the tithes into the storehouse…[and if you do] I will open the windows of heaven for you. I will pour out a blessing so great you won't have enough room to take it in! Try it! Put me to the test!" (Mal. 3:10, NLT).

Fourth, we both acknowledged the biblical truth that if you want to get a harvest, you have to plant some seed.

In Luke 6:38 Jesus said, "Give, and it will be given to you. A good measure, pressed down, shaken together and running over, will be poured into your lap. For with the measure you use, it will be measured to you." The Scripture does not say, "Pray and it will be given you," but "*Give*, and it will be given to you." It goes without saying that we must pray about everything, but in this specific teaching about giving, Jesus uses *giving* as a synonym for *planting*.

We had many cotton farmers in our Texas church, and I never heard one of them ask for prayer that they would have a crop. No, they planted their seed first and then prayed. Planting always comes before harvest. And giving always comes before receiving.

Fifth, we promised each other that even if our finances were down, we would never speak of our need to others or hint around that we couldn't afford this or that. Nor would we make a prayer request of our finances, using this as a backdoor method to arouse people's sympathies.

In short and in summary, before we ever reached the borders of Texas, Marilee and I determined that God would be our Source.

And that is exactly what has transpired through the years. In the following paragraphs, I offer three brief examples (chosen out of many) of His faithfulness to provide for us in miraculous ways.

Exactly What We Needed

A few short weeks after we arrived, we faced our first test.

As a result of our move from California to Texas, we found ourselves with a $350 deficit in funds. Praying a similar prayer to the one King Jehoshaphat laid before the Lord in 2 Chronicles 20:12, we said, "We don't know what to do (about the $350), but our eyes are upon You."

The answer came in a most unusual way. Two couples of our church invited Marilee and me to go to Lubbock for dinner, and on our way home we stopped at a Dairy Queen as we were leaving the town. I was asking Billy and Dick, both cotton farmers, questions about farming. How many acres is the average cotton farm? How many bales of cotton do you get per acre? How much is a bale of cotton worth?

The men were having a good laugh about this new pastor and his wife from Los Angeles and the culture shock we must be experiencing to find ourselves in a small farming town in Texas. One of them said to the other, "To show Paul and Marilee appreciation for coming to be our pastor, why don't we each give them a bale of cotton?"

A bale of cotton at that time was worth $175, and they each wrote out a check. That night Marilee and I sat down at the kitchen table, looking at those checks, absolutely amazed by God's faithfulness and the generosity of His people. It was exactly the $350 we had prayed for.

PROVISION UPON PROVISION

R. J. Walls was a former pastor of our Texas church who had gone into business, enjoyed success, and found his niche as a generous benefactor to the kingdom of God. Some time after we arrived, R. J. and his wife, Faye, took an interest in Marilee and me and would come down from Lubbock to visit our church about once a month.

They would take us out for dinner, and before they left R. J. would put a one hundred dollar bill in my hand and would say each time, "You're sure doing a good job. God's hand is on you, and He's preparing you for a wonderful future. God has great plans for you. We're sure proud of you!"

Of course, the money was a huge blessing to us, reminding us of Jesus' "Give and it shall be given unto you" promise. As time went on, however, we came to realize that the Walls' fellowship and encouragement—beyond anything they ever gave us—was like pure gold.

The generosity of the church through the years of our pastorate was overwhelming. They took care of us like we were family. We would return from a vacation to find new furniture in our home. There were always unexpected gifts that seemed to come just when we needed them most. As time went on, the church dug deeper, increasing our salary. They were most generous beyond belief.

As much as the Texans may have adopted the Rissers, however, they never did accept our Volkswagen Bug. We found that Texans didn't like anything small, especially cars. They would either laugh or cringe when they saw our little Bug around town. A number of them didn't want *their* pastor representing them in a Beetle. As a result, some of the men of the church helped us to get a larger car, more in keeping with a Texan.

One day I walked into the state bank in our town. Sitting in the board room were three of the most influential men of the community: Bruce Zorns, the bank president; Al Muldrow, a former Texas Secretary of State; and Grady Goodpasture, founder and owner of a conglomerate of businesses that extended all the way to Houston.

I knew them all very well, so they invited me into the office to sit with them. None of them was from our church. During the conversation they expressed appreciation for the dynamics of our church and expressed appreciation for the church's contribution to the town.

On the spot they determined to make a contribution to be split between the church and Marilee and me. So they each put two thousand dollars into our personal and church accounts. What an above-and-beyond gift from three of the makers and shakers of our town! Their affirmation meant the world to all of us.

AND AS TO THE EDUCATION OF OUR CHILDREN...

I feel no ill will toward my old boss, with all his dire predictions of the Rissers' pending financial doom. However, I do recognize his words for what they were: It was Satan's attempt to steal our optimism and joy by casting doubt on the willingness and ability of God to take care of and provide for our family.

Shaking a finger in my face, he had warned, "You are on the road to financial ruin, from which you will never recover... There is no way you'll be able to provide for your children's education."

The Lord, however, had the last word on that matter, too.

Brad, our oldest son, graduated from West Point and then received a master's degree from Pepperdine University. Mike earned a degree in business administration from the University of Southern California. Terry attended California State University, Fullerton, and LIFE Bible College, with an MDiv from Fuller Theological Seminary.

We returned to Southern California from that imagined "road to ruin" with an undaunted belief in God's faithfulness and His ability to provide in every situation of life.

CHAPTER 9

EVERY DETAIL OF OUR LIVES

S HIRLEY VIALL, A LONGTIME member of our church, approached me a couple of years ago at the conclusion of a memorial service.

"Pastor," she said, "did I ever tell you the end of the story regarding our conversation we had in your office many years ago?"

My first thought was, "What story?" I asked her to jog my memory, because we had counseled at different times on different subjects. When I found out that this particular conversation and counseling session had taken place over fifteen years before, I felt better about my memory!

Shirley reminded me of the situation at that time. Her husband had just left her and her young daughter and was under a court order to pay her child support.

That brought the memory back to me. This man had been so vindictive and bitter that he refused to pay so much as a penny—even if it meant he would go to jail. (Thankfully, the laws on child support are much stiffer than they were in those days.) My first instinct was to tell her to let him stay in jail for a few months and perhaps that might help him change his mind. Her heartfelt remarks in that moment, however, stopped me in my tracks.

"Pastor, I don't want to go to court against the father of my daughter. I can't take the emotional stress. I can handle the loss of child support easier than I can deal with a court battle and lawsuit." She went on to note that the Lord had given her a good-paying job and that she could make it without child support. She would leave the problem in the Lord's hands and count on Him completely to bring her through.

But what advice had I given her that day? For the life of me, I couldn't remember what I had told her.

With a smile, Shirley again reminded me.

"You said, 'If you're trying to avert trouble and put the issue in the God's hands, why don't you consider the money you are forfeiting as His and that you are doing this "as unto the Lord."'"

"That's what I told you?"

"Yes, and then you quoted from Colossians 3:23–24." She opened her Bible and read, "Work willingly at whatever you do, as though you were working for the Lord rather than for people. Remember that the Lord will give you an inheritance as your reward, and that the Master you are serving is Christ" (NLT).

In that way, I apparently told her, she wouldn't have to be troubled by the knowledge that she was being unfairly short-changed by a bitter man. Instead, it could be an act of devotion and an evidence that all she was and all she had belonged to Jesus and that He would care for her.

She updated me by letting me know that her ex-husband had died several years ago. I hadn't known that. She also told me that her former father-in-law, who had also died, had been deeply ashamed and angered by the way his son had treated her. He had apologized for his son's conduct and told her he was leaving her a substantial sum of money to her in his will. Her father-in-law was true to his word, leaving her a generous endowment at his passing.

But here is where the story gets even better.

"Pastor," she said, "when my ex-husband refused to give me the child support, I was making a good salary and made it without him. But now I'm without a job or income, and, at the time I needed it most, God provided for me. I always wondered how I would make it when I got older, and I could never come up with an answer. I had often worried about it, but God had a plan all along."

Her eyes were shining as she said, "Isn't the Lord great?"

More recently, Shirley told me about purchasing a home. It had always been her desire to buy a house, but she had told the Lord to take that desire away if home ownership wasn't part of His plan for her.

But the desire never left her. Finally, just before her father-in-law died, she had found a home she could afford, even though she had no money left over to furnish and decorate it.

Then came the money from the will which amounted to far more than the husband's child support would have been. This enabled her to decorate her home in the manner she had dreamed of for so many years.

"God even cares about the little things, doesn't He?" she smiled.

I had to agree, remembering the words of the psalmist in Psalm 37:23, "He delights in every detail of [our] lives" (NLT).

CHAPTER 10

TERRY'S PAPER ROUTE

GOD KNOWS AND CARES about all the things that are important to us. He performs miracles in the simplest of situations, if our eyes are open to recognize them.

One Saturday evening I came home from a day of preparation for Sunday. As I walked through the house to go to my room to change clothes, I walked past the room of our youngest son, Terry. He and his mother were having a serious conversation. I stopped with the intention to fix whatever was wrong. But, before I could fix it I needed to know what to fix.

Marilee told me, "We're just talking." Then she explained that Terry was going to deliver thirty newspapers on our middle son's paper route the next morning. Terry knew the route well, but there was one problem. The route covered thirty-one homes. The paper was delivered every day of the week, but there was one family who didn't take the Sunday paper. Because Terry had never delivered on Sunday, he didn't know which customer that was.

I should have been spiritually alert, but my brilliant logic was at the forefront. I knew I could fix things. My solution was that the next morning I would go over to the newspaper dispenser and buy a paper. Then Terry could throw one to each house. The problem was solved! "You don't have to worry anymore," I reassured them, quite pleased with my fix.

Marilee wasn't impressed. She told me that they weren't worrying and that she wanted to teach him to pray. I, too, wanted him to learn to pray, but I also wanted our boys to be logical.

She insisted, "This time just let me do it my way."

Early the next morning when I was ready to leave for church, I offered once more to buy a paper, but they turned down my offer. They prayed again before Terry went out the door. I decided to delay my departure until he returned, thinking I still might have to take him to buy a paper. I had the coins ready in my pocket.

In a short time Terry returned full of excitement. He told us how he came to a house where a man came out in his robe. As Terry started to throw the paper, the man said, "No. Remember, I don't take the Sunday paper." Terry said this was the only person who was outside during his whole route. Terry and Marilee hugged each other, leaving me out of the circle.

In the process of Terry learning a lesson about God's faithfulness to answer prayer and provide a small miracle to do it, I also learned a lesson: God even cares about paper routes.

But I still think my idea was rather brilliant.

CHAPTER 11

WHEN THINGS HAVE GONE TOO FAR

I HAVE A VERY SPECIAL friend who grew up in a home where his dad, in particular, was dead-set against religion of all kinds. As a result, the family never participated in anything spiritual.

As a boy, Mark had a very close relationship with his mother and was devastated by her sudden death when he was only ten years old. Multiplying that heartbreak a hundred times over, his dad remarried to a woman who disliked Mark. He remembers staying away from home at nights—even at a young age—to avoid a bad encounter with his stepmother. After he saw that all the lights were out, he would sneak back into the house and into his bed.

When he was fifteen, Mark went to church with one of his friends and received Christ into his life. For all his happiness over believing in Jesus as Lord and Savior, however, Mark recalls that his conversion had a very difficult side, too. He was grateful and happy to have an assurance of going to heaven when he died, but what about his mother? She had never received Jesus as Savior. It was hard for Mark to even contemplate being in heaven without her. He agonized over that thought for days, but finally faced the fact he could do nothing about it.

Mark went on to serve the Lord, and after high school

enrolled at LIFE Bible College. He commuted to work, home, and college, maintaining a rather busy schedule.

One day when he was returning home from a long day of classes, Mrs. Bell, the Christian neighbor from across the street, called out to Mark, asking him about his busy life and all his comings and goings. Mark told her of how he had become a Christian a couple years before and was now attending LIFE Bible College.

Mrs. Bell's face lit up with a joyful radiance, and then she gave him the shock of his life. "Oh, Mark," she said, "*your mother would be so proud of you!*"

What a strange remark! Mark's father was a secular Jew and was resistant to any faith. Mark's mother had gone to a church in her childhood in Indiana, where spiritual seed was planted in her being. Yet, while living with her secular husband, she never made waves, so she never pursued her faith. In retrospect, Mark saw them as a lost cause. But suddenly it appeared to him that those early teachings had made his mother receptive to the gospel when it was presented to her as an adult.

Mrs. Bell's words were as news from heaven to Mark.

Seeing the puzzled look on his face, she said, "Mark, didn't you know your mother used to come to my house with a group of women in the neighborhood, and we were all praying for her. I remember the day your mother received Christ as her Savior! This was a great answer to our prayers. She assured us that if she died, she had eternal life. She never told your dad because she knew he would stop her from being with us, but we all remember the day she trusted in Christ."

For a moment or two, Mark could only stand there in Mrs. Bell's driveway trying to absorb these best-of-all tidings. In that instant, it was as though darkness had become light and death had become life. *He would see his mother again!*

As I've pondered Mark's story, I love to reflect on that reassuring passage in Romans 8 that asserts how the Holy Spirit not only prays with us but prays *for* us.

> And the Holy Spirit helps us in our weakness. For example, we don't know what God wants us to pray for. But the Holy Spirit prays for us with groanings that cannot be expressed in words. And the Father who knows all hearts knows what the Spirit is saying, for the Spirit pleads for us believers in harmony with God's own will.
>
> —ROMANS 8:26–27

In situations like Mark Simon's, I often wonder if the Holy Spirit Himself is praying for certain outcomes, certain deep heart's desires, before we're even aware that such things are possible. One thing I've learned for sure: He's always working behind the scenes to bring blessing and help to God's children.

Several years before Mark's stepmother, who had tried to keep Mark, his wife, and children apart from Mark's father, died. This gave the opportunity for the entire Simon family to be gloriously united, though Mark's dad only had a short time to live. The family was on a mission to make sure that this man would receive the Lord before he died.

Casey, Mark's young daughter, turned out to be the point person in that mission, since she was her grandfather's pride and joy. Casey told her grandpa that it was vital for him to put his faith in the Lord so that he would go to heaven. He, with tears, told the family he didn't want to go anywhere his first wife, Mark's mother, would not be. That's when Casey shared with him the great good news that his wife had received Christ at Mrs. Bell's home across the street and that Grandma was already in heaven. Mark's father cried for relief and joy, yielded his own life to Jesus, and experienced a genuine conversion.

The Bible makes it clear in Luke 15 that the lost sheep, lost coin, and lost son are all representative of lost-and-found people. The Bible says that the angels of heaven rejoice over each sinner who comes to Christ. Imagine how loved ones—in heaven and on Earth—feel about those who were thought to be lost but come into the kingdom at the last moment.

Chapter 12

Rosie's Story

ROSIE CAME TO OUR church from the Los Angeles Mission. She testified of her wonderful conversion.

She had been on the street, a homeless, alcoholic drug addict, making the little money she could get by selling herself. Her only shelter was in a burned and rusted-out car shell in an empty lot right across the street from the house where she had grown up and where her parents still lived with her three children. She had lost custody of the little ones and had stolen so much from her parents that they had given up on her and refused to let her come into the house.

Rosie's assessment of herself was that she had reached a point as low and worthless as a human being could get. "I was a hard, mean, ugly, person," she recalled. "Untouchable! I stunk so bad I couldn't stand myself and would go weeks on end without a shower. I really didn't care about anything. I was as hard and heartless as a rock."

But no more! She sobbed as she described how she went into a Los Angeles mission for a donut.

"Marsha, one of the leaders at the mission came up to me and put her arms around me and told me she loved me. I melted. For the first time in my life I felt important. And something strange went through my mind. Yes, it was Marsha who loved me, but I really had the feeling that it was God who hugged me. Miraculously, every bit of bitterness, sinfulness, worthlessness drained out of me; and for the first time in my life, I was glad to be a black lady. I was now at peace with myself.

"Later on that morning I was able to take a shower. But, I had already been cleansed by the blood and love of Christ, and today I am a new woman in Christ Jesus. I felt important."

Rosie was restored to her parents and children and is now a supervisor of a Christian restoration home for homeless women.

CHAPTER 13

SOMETHING CHANGED
HIS LIFE!

Because I became good friends with Dr. Overton
two years ago and was so captivated by his story
and his life, I wanted to include this mention of
him in the book.

N OT MANY CONVERSION STORIES make it to the pages of
the *Wall Street Journal,* but Dr. Marvin Overton's did.

A June 6, 1994 article by Robert Johnson shows how true it is
that when a person accepts Christ all things become new.*

At the time of the *Wall Street Journal* account, Dr. Overton
was one of the finest brain surgeons in the nation and a past
president of the Texas Association of Neurosurgeons. In 1992,
through a series of curious circumstances, he began attending
a small church in Burnet, Texas, and experienced a spiritual
awakening.

At about the same time, however, he began suffering severe,
lingering pains in his abdomen. Subsequent x-rays eventually
revealed cancer. Several days after the initial diagnosis, however,

---

* Robert Johnson, "Dr. Martin Overton," *The Wall Street Journal,*
June 6, 1994.

tests revealed *nothing at all.* Dr. Overton was completely healed, every symptom vanished, and that dramatic miracle crystallized his born-again experience.

Before his conversion, he was a skeptic and a rationalist who believed in the power of science. Now, as the *Journal* reported, Overton has "More answers than questions, a granite certitude about the mind, the brain, and the soul."

Before his conversion his god was wine. Not that he was an alcoholic. In fact, he owned one of the finest wine collections in America—over ten thousand bottles of every important vintage made between the late 1700s and 1930—worth more than a million dollars. Dr. Overton threw wine-tasting banquets attended by French chefs flown in by Concorde jets.

"Wine had become my idol," Overton admitted. "I worshiped the god Bacchus. I was an excellent heathen." After Overton's conversion he sold his wine collection, giving much of the proceeds to charity.

Before his conversion, Overton was a Ft. Worth socialite. Now he is one of the leaders in his small-town, blue-collar church in Burnet, Texas. He even goes door to door to tell others about Christ.

What impressed others most was not his healing but his life. "The question of whether he got an incorrect diagnosis or whatever, really doesn't matter," said Michael McWhorter, chairman of the American Association of Neurological Surgeons Science Board. "Who are we to say a miracle didn't happen? *Something* changed his life."

CHAPTER 14

DIVINE INDICATORS— SIGNS AND EVIDENCES

FINDING A PRODIGAL DAUGHTER

ELLEN AGONIZED OVER THE spiritual lostness of her daughter, who in her youth had walked faithfully with the Lord. In her late teens, the young woman had rejected her spiritual moorings, defying almost everything in her life that was good, righteous, and principled.

She had become a prodigal.

Ellen, of course, prayed for her daughter every day and tried to stay connected through phone calls and cards.

Soon, they lost even that connection. Calls went unanswered, phone numbers were changed, and letters seemed to disappear into the void. It now seemed like an impenetrable wall separated mother and daughter.

Months went by without a word. It broke Ellen's heart not to know where her daughter was or how she was getting along. Not knowing what else to do, she persisted in prayer, every day, every night, whispering her hurt, desires, and longings to the Lord.

Even though she had been a leader and Bible teacher in her church and was a woman of strong faith, Ellen felt cold fingers of doubt touch her heart. She had stopped praying for something dramatic and supernatural to happen in her relationship with her daughter and decided to pray for something small.

She told the Lord she trusted Him and had the capacity to "wait upon the Lord" as long as needed. But she dared to ask her Lord if He would give her an indication—some small sign—that He had heard her heartbroken prayers.

"Lord," she prayed, "I'm not looking for a quick resolution here; just a sign that You've heard me and that You're working."

Later that very morning, a van from a local florist pulled into Ellen's driveway. The delivery person came to the front door with a small bouquet of flowers and a note: "Hi, Mom. I love you."

It was signed by her daughter.

No, the daughter hadn't come home or even indicated where she was or what had been happening in her life.

But Ellen had prayed for an indicator, and she had most certainly received one, almost immediately. Her heart flooded with joy and wonder. This was, to Ellen, like Elijah's cloud "the size of a man's hand." In that Old Testament account, the prophet had seen that tiny cloud over the ocean and knew his prayer for rain—a big, heavy rain—had been answered. (See 1 Kings 18:41–45.)

She prayed more diligently than ever before, and soon the full answer came. Mother and daughter were reunited—emotionally, geographically, and spiritually.

TO MOVE OR NOT TO MOVE

In my former leadership position within our denomination, I became acquainted with one of the top bankers in the nation. I was delighted to discover that he was a committed Christian, living his life humbly and in daily dependence on the Lord.

In the course of one of our conversations, my friend asked for my input and prayer about a decision that would be critical not only for his career but for his entire family. His firm was asking him to take a new position, which would mean relocating from the East Coast to the West Coast.

While no one disputed that this would be dramatic new opportunity for his banking career, he also understood that it could be a major cultural shock for his family. He and his wife and Christian friends had put all the "minuses and plusses" on the ledger, but it really boiled down to this: What did the Lord want him to do? After all, only God knew their future, knew them, and knew what would be best for them in the years to come.

"Only God knows sees the entire picture," he told me. "I really need His direction."

Because he himself was responsible for relocating banking executives all over the country—and even overseas—he well understood how upsetting such a major move could be. On the one hand, it could be good for the whole family. On the other hand, he had seen ill-conceived relocations cause ship-wrecks for marriages and families. He didn't want his decision to end in tragedy and didn't want to sacrifice his children in the interest of his banking career.

He told me later that after he and his wife had prayed through the whole process, they had come to this conclusion: the move had to be a positive for their two daughters, one who would be entering sixth grade and another, the younger of the two, going into second grade.

He and I talked about asking God for an indicator or sign that they were moving in the right direction. A colleague in Los

Angeles had told him that if he moved into the area, he needed to get his girls into a certain top-notch Christian school. But he also added that it would be difficult because the school always had a long waiting list.

He and I agreed that situation could give us the divine indicator we'd been looking for. If he could miraculously get both his girls enrolled in that school at such a late date, it would be a sign from the Lord, and they could consider it a green light to move ahead.

The banker flew into Los Angeles on the weekend, and first thing Monday morning he went to the school to check the status of any vacancies. He later confessed to me that as he pulled into the school's campus that morning, his expectations were low. In fact, he was preparing himself for disappointment and telling himself he needed to be satisfied with the job he already had. (Even though it would mean forfeiting a major promotion!)

The principal knew he was coming, but because of what she perceived was a full enrollment, she let him know they had reached their capacity. She was so doubtful of any openings that she hadn't even bothered to ask the banker what grades his girls were in. Sitting across her desk from him, she glanced through the latest report from the registrar. She had been away the previous Friday and was puzzled by two new entries. Apparently, two families who had been previously enrolled had suddenly moved out of the area. "The school is essentially at full capacity," she was saying, "except for these two new vacancies I'm seeing for the first time here, one in second grade and one in the sixth."

The banker could hardly believe his ears. "But those are the grades of my girls!" he said.

That was the divine green light he had been looking for! To California they came, convinced of the truth contained in David's words:

> The Lord directs the steps of the godly. He delights in
> every detail of their lives.
> —Psalm 37:23, NLT

A few months after the move, I spoke with the banker again, who happily reported they were settled and prospering. In fact, they were so happy in their new locale that he and his wife had looked at each other across the breakfast table that very morning and said to each other, "Why didn't we move here years ago?"

CHAPTER 15

IRWIN'S VISION

FOR YEARS, IRWIN BARNETT was the production manager of the famous TV game program *The Price Is Right*, with the legendary Bob Barker. Despite his success, however, Irwin had become so depressed with life that he went to the president of CBS Studios, Michael Klausman, and asked for a six-week leave of absence.

Mike is a committed Christian and was a member of my church at that time. In Mike's office that day, Irwin unraveled his whole sad and hopeless story. He was trapped in a sinful, destructive lifestyle that seemingly had no escape. He had a full-blown case of AIDS and was giving serious thought to taking his own life.

Mike realized that this was more than a request for a leave of absence; it was a desperate cry for help. He asked me to find someone in the area who would lead Irwin to Christ, nurture him in the faith, and get him plugged into a church.

I immediately thought of Dr. Harold Helms of Angelus Temple. With characteristic kindness and compassion, Dr. Helms explained the gospel message to Irwin, who reached out for it like a drowning man grasping for a life preserver.

The next step was obvious. Dr. Helms called on Leita Mae Stewart, the best disciple-maker he knew, to take on spiritual responsibility for Irwin and to teach him in the ways of the Lord.

Sometime later, Irwin gave an account of his transformational conversion. The vision he had of himself at that time was a man neck-deep in a gross, putrid cesspool, and sinking by the moment. But the moment Irwin called out to the Lord Jesus for help, Jesus reached down to him and pulled him out of that rancid pit. In Irwin's vision, two things happened in that moment. First, he was instantly cleansed of all the filth he had been sinking in and found himself absolutely pure and clean. Second, as Jesus waded into the pit and pulled him out, none of the filth touched Him at all; He remained perfectly clean and holy.

After his conversion, he had the calm, joyful assurance that he had been washed clean by the blood of Christ. He knew (and knew that he knew) that his sins would never again be held against him. I don't know of anyone who loved the truth of Romans 8:1 more than Irwin Barnett: "Therefore, there is now no condemnation for those who are in Christ Jesus."

Irwin set his heart on being a productive follower of Christ and making his life count during the years he had to live. Many were praying for his healing from AIDS, but this never took place.

One of the ministries he undertook was teaching a Bible study during the noon hour at CBS Studios. At its height, there were more than sixty people in attendance. Some twenty-five people, most of them employees at CBS, found the Lord and learned to walk with the Lord through Irwin's dynamic and faithful ministry.

What a story! Here was a man who, by his own account,

had lived a "ruinous, wasted, sinful life" that reached such low depths that he determined to commit suicide, but the Lord reached down and redeemed him, giving him a new chance in his earthly life and destining him for eternal life.

Two or three weeks before his passing, Irwin asked me to conduct his funeral, which I gladly agreed to do. When we sat down to talk about it, I asked him what he wanted said.

Here are some of the thoughts he wanted verbalized after he had departed for a new life in the Father's house.

- "Tell them that I regret my sinful lifestyle. Until I gave my life to God, I had wasted my one opportunity to be something special. In that sense, I wish I had my life to live over. I would certainly live it differently.

- "The greatest thing that ever happened to me was when Christ came into my life, lifted me out of my cesspool of sin, and made me a new person. The Bible says, "If anyone is in Christ, he is a new creation; the old has gone, the new has come!" (2 Cor. 5:17). Jesus truly redeemed my life from destruction.

- "God gave me the opportunity of making the most of my life after I gave myself to Him. I had always sought for meaning in my life but couldn't find it until I found Christ. I was continually trying to find purpose, but, foolish me, I was so spiritually blind that I had no idea that my purpose would be found in the most unlikely Person—in knowing God Himself. Similarly, I desperately sought to be happy, but

I couldn't comprehend what happiness even was until I found Christ. He gave me overwhelming happiness that is indescribable.

- "At certain stages of my life, I had made feeble attempts to find God. But then I discovered that God had been attempting to find me!

- "My death is a consequence for living life my way. But now, even though I am dying, I have eternal life before me because of Christ's death on the cross—because Christ was willing to live *His* life God's way. That is why I can say, 'For me, to live is Christ and to die is gain' (Phil. 1:21).

- "If you don't know me well, you might be apt to say that 'Irwin turned into a religious nut.' But if you do know my background, you will know that I was a nut *before* I came to myself and gave my life to the Lord. I was a nut for Satan, living a life of destruction and emptiness on a road leading to a dead end.

- "God has turned my sorrow into joy, my mourning into dancing, and my emptiness into fullness. He has turned me from despair to hope, from darkness to light, and from eternal damnation to eternal life. With everything that is in me, I pray that if you don't know God, today You will make a decision to accept Him and live for Him. *Jesus is the answer!*"

CHAPTER 16

HIDING IN THE BALCONY

A YOUNG COUPLE IN WICHITA, Kansas—he seventeen and she sixteen—had eloped and just returned from their honeymoon. When they attended their Sunday morning church service, their pastor sent out a stern warning to his congregants.

"This week there is going to be a revival crusade at the civic auditorium. It's going to be led by a Jezebel, Aimee Simple McPherson, and I don't want anyone from my church to attend."

The new wife turned to her husband and whispered, "What's a Jez-a-bel?"

"I don't know," he said. "But let's go and find out."

They went and sat in the upper balcony as far as one could be from the pulpit in order to avoid being seen by their church members. At the end of the service, the evangelist was about to pray the benediction when she delayed for a moment. She asked the audience if they would give her a moment because she knew that the Holy Spirit was speaking to a young couple in the balcony. "God wants to use them in a special way," she said, "and they're going to make the decision to surrender to Him before they leave tonight. God is speaking to them *right now,* and they *will* come down the aisle and meet me as I prepare to close this service."

The couple looked at each other and simultaneously said, "She's talking about us!"

With trepidation, they went down the stairway and then down the aisle to meet with Mrs. McPherson, committing themselves to Christ and answering God's call to His service and ministry. In just five weeks' time, Harold and Ione Jeffries were in Los Angeles preparing for ministry.

The Jefferies went on to have a long-term pastorate in Portland, Oregon, that touched the world. During a Portland Crusade in which Dr. Jeffries served as chairman, the great evangelist Billy Graham referred to him as one of the most outstanding pastors in America.

Dr. Jeffries' church, Portland Foursquare, became the seedbed of the outstanding growth of our denomination in the Pacific Northwest. Out of the congregation came a large number of pastors and missionaries who went on to impact the world.

But it all started with two newlyweds who ignored their pastor's stern warning and went to "see the Jezebel."

CHAPTER 17

A TOUGH MISSIONARY
FOUND IN A SNOWBANK

A SEVERE AND PROLONGED SNOWSTORM totally paralyzed all forms of transportation in Portland, Oregon, on that unforgettable Sunday night in February 1937.

Over two feet of snow had fallen, making driving—or even walking—all but impossible. Mrs. Jeffries, the wife of Dr. Harold Jeffries and co-pastor of the Portland Foursquare Church, was scheduled to bring the sermon that evening.

"I really don't know what to do," she remarked to her husband. "The Lord gave me a message for non-Christians, and no one will be at church other than the church members that live nearby."

"Hon," Dr. Jeffries replied, "God knew this terrible storm was coming. So if He's laid this message on your heart, you should preach it just as God gave it to you."

With great effort, the Jefferies made their way to the church to minister to the few who would be present. What they didn't know was that two blocks away from the church, a beer truck was snowbound, and the driver was sitting with his wife in the cab. Seeing the lights of the church, the couple decided to brave the storm and at least get inside, where there would be some warmth from the cold.

They sat in the back of the church sanctuary, where the

service proceeded. After the singing and prayer, Mrs. Jefferies brought the message the Holy Spirit had given her. When she finished she gave an invitation for those who didn't know the Lord to receive Christ.

Two hands went up in the back row—those of the beer truck driver and his wife, Joe and Virginia Knapp. The Knapps experienced a genuine conversion that freezing winter night, and their lives were never the same.

Two weeks later Joe Knapp asked the pastor, "Dr. Jefferies, do you think a person can be a Christian and drive a beer truck?"

"Well, Joe," he said, "what do *you* think?"

"I'm resigning my job tomorrow morning," he declared, "and trusting God to take care of us." It was a big decision in those difficult days of the 1930s, but God was faithful and did indeed take good care of the Knapps.

Tough, burly Joe Knapp had not only been a leading bootlegger in the city but had taken on the role of "head goon" in enforcing the will of the local Teamsters union. No one ever thought Joe Knapp and his wife would ever do an about-face in life—let alone become a dedicated Christian couple.

Joe had a great desire to win others to Christ. One evening after the church service, he came upon a crowd. There before his eyes a man was beating his wife.

Joe turned to the crowd and demanded, "Is anybody going to help that woman?"

When there was no response, Joe plunged himself into the situation, put a double hammerlock on the man, and marched him toward the church and prayer chapel, telling someone to bring the pastor. When Dr. Jefferies entered the chapel, Joe had the man pinned to the floor and said, "Dr. Jefferies, this man wants to get saved!"

As Dr. Jeffries presented the claims of Christ to this captive audience, the man was converted. He and his wife became members of the church. It was Joe's first convert, and he acknowledged that he needed to work on his methods. They were still just a little bit rough.

Joe and Virginia enrolled in the Portland Bible School, and later finished their training at LIFE Bible College in Los Angeles. With a call upon their hearts to be missionaries, they were soon on their way to a ministry in Panama. After a number of fruitful years there, they moved on to the nation of Colombia, where God used them to build the largest Protestant church in that nation—even in an era of intense opposition and persecution.

It was through the Knapps' ministry that the noted missionaries John and Jean Firth were baptized with the Holy Spirit, launching yet another tidal wave of ministry that went on for years with great results.

But it all began on a dark and snowy night in Portland when Mrs. Jeffries chose to obey the Holy Spirit and preach an evangelistic message to a (nearly) empty sanctuary.

Chapter 18

Unconventional Conversions

John

J OHN WAS IN THE air force, and when a Christian officer took the time to explain the way of salvation to him, he listened politely. (It was always a good idea to be courteous to officers!)

As their conversation concluded, he told the Christian man that he wasn't ready to make that commitment, but he would think about it until they met again.

After that encounter, John had some leave days coming and went to visit at his parents' home. His aunt happened to be staying with them at the time, and late one night she and John had a long talk at the kitchen table after his parents had retired for the night.

The grief and desolation in his aunt's heart took John completely by surprise. With growing alarm, he listened as she poured out her innermost pain. She was depressed, had lost her will to live, and was frankly at the end of her rope. She didn't know where to turn.

Remarkably, John had a clear memory of everything the Christian officer back at the base had told him about the Lord. He shared the plan of salvation with her as it had been explained to him. He told her that if she invited Christ to come into her life, He would forgive all her sins, impart His very nature to her, and give her new desires. God Himself, he told her, would give her the joy and purpose for living that she wanted so deeply.

"But how do I do it?" she asked.

Once again drawing on his memory of the conversation with the officer, he explained how she could offer her life to the Lord, ask for His forgiveness and cleansing, and ask Him to come into her life and become her Savior.

The next morning when his aunt came down to breakfast, John immediately knew that something had happened. This was a different woman from the one he had talked to the previous night. She excitedly let him know that something extraordinary had happened to her after she prayed before going to bed. It was like a huge load had been lifted from her spirit, and she was flooded with peace. Everything was different, and how could she thank John enough for showing her the way?

She went on from that day to live a totally new life.

Not long after that experience, John was converted himself. After his time in the military, he served on a pastoral staff and had the opportunity to share his faith in Christ with many, many people.

But he had led his first person to the Lord before he ever accepted the Lord himself!

THE GOSPEL HAS POWER

> His purpose was for the nations to seek after God and perhaps feel their way toward him and find him— though he is not far from any one of us.
>
> —ACTS 17:27, NLT

Tom Paterson became a friend of many of us when he served as a strategic planner for our denomination. He was one of the closest friends of and coauthor with the late Peter Drucker, recognized as one of the greatest minds in the world on business management. Both of them, committed Christians, used their experience and findings to bless churches by teaching them to maximize their resources, financially and personnel-wise.

Tom was sent to China by President Reagan to introduce their Marxist economic leaders to a market economy. He was cautioned not to say anything about Christianity, God, or things spiritual. He followed their high-handed restrictions, but he prayed that what he was unable to speak he would be able to show.

Tom found great joy in telling how at the end of almost every seminar people would line up to speak to him. After every meeting, without fail, someone would say in broken English, "I a Christian too," obviously insinuating they could tell Tom was a Christian.

I recently called Tom at his home in Oregon to ask him to help me recall an almost unbelievable account of an experience in China.

His favorite experience came after one meeting when everyone left, except one of their leaders, and he identified himself as a Christian. Tom asked, "How did you become a Christian?"

He told how in China they required everyone who was going to interface with Americans to take university tracks that would familiarize them with American life, such as language, thinking processes, lifestyles, values/priorities, even to the point of learning the religion of America, Christianity.

The atheist professor of Western religion chose to teach Christianity with sarcasm, so as he taught the essentials of Christianity he did so sneeringly, explaining how the central figure of Christianity is Jesus Christ. "He is the Messiah, who Christians claim to be the Son of God. At the end of His life He died like a criminal, crucified on a cross. In doing so His blood would wash away the evil of bad people. And by receiving Jesus into your being you will have eternal life." He added that "the biggest hoax is the claim that Jesus resurrected from the dead, which is celebrated on their most religious day of the year: Easter." Many were laughing derisively, while others seemed to be pondering.

The leader told how we went to his apartment after that lecture and prayed as best he knew, asking God to help him be a Christian. Later, he was able to buy a Bible, and soon he began to notice a real change in his life. His values and character were transformed. He told Tom that he had gone from being a person who was empty on the inside to having found the purpose for life. "I feel full!" he happily added. To show off his knowledge of Scripture he proclaimed, "I have been *born again!*"

I talked to Tom Paterson this week to recount all aspects of that experience. Tom was inspired just to relive that exciting experience. He raised his voice almost to a shout as he exclaimed, "Paul, that shows the power of the gospel!"

To that I say, "Amen!"

Those of us who preach must take our role seriously, but it is imperative that we realize that the real power is in the message. This why the apostle said:

> For I am not ashamed of this Good News about Christ.
> It is the power of God at work, saving everyone who

believes—the Jew first and also the Gentile. This Good News tells us how God makes us right in his sight. This is accomplished from start to finish by faith. As the Scriptures say, "It is through faith that a righteous person has life."

—ROMANS 1:16, NLT

CHAPTER 19

DRAWN BY JOY

ONE SUNDAY MORNING AT the close of a church service, when almost everyone was gone, one of our lady elders asked me if I would talk with a newcomer who had given her heart to the Lord.

She was wearing sunglasses, which I concluded immediately were for the purpose of concealing black eyes and a bruised face. I also noticed that she was crying uncontrollably, in a most unusual way that you seem only to see when the Holy Spirit is doing a special work in a person's heart. Yes, she was sobbing over a tragedy in her life, for sure. But there was another emotion mixed in, almost of relief.

After we talked for a couple minutes, her story began to emerge. She explained that she lived just over the freeway from the church. On the previous night, she and her husband had engaged in a vicious argument that ended in an all-out husband–wife brawl in which she was thoroughly beat up, accounting for all the facial bruises. She admitted, however, that the argument and the physical violence had been as much hers as his. Finally, in a rage, her husband had thrown some clothes into a bag, got into their only car, and drove away cursing her.

"The next time I see you," he snarled, "will probably be in hell."

Immediately aware that she was as responsible for the fight

as he was, she had wept until she had no strength left to weep. She had tried to pray, but she was sure she was so far from God He would never hear her.

Or had He?

Throughout the course of the sleepless night that followed, she had felt a strong and deepening need for the Lord.

She decided that her first step toward God should be toward the church. The only church she knew about, however, was the traditional church she had grown up in as a child, never attending as an adult. She got out of bed, put on her makeup to try to cover the bruises, put on a nice dress, and started walking toward the church.

The path to her church, however, took her past our church. As she walked, she noticed bunches of people making their way to our service from their parking spaces on a nearby street.

She said she couldn't help but notice all the children skipping and laughing with one another and how the adults seemed so joyful. It didn't make sense to her. Why were all these people so happy about going to church? She was impressed with their excitement, remembering how she had dreaded going to church as a child and couldn't wait for the day when she was old enough that she didn't have to go anymore. It was, as she remembered it, the most boring hour in the week.

But the people on the sidewalk heading to church that morning didn't seem to be bored at all. In fact, they seemed excited, filled with anticipation.

As a result, instead of continuing down the street to the church she had intended to attend that day, she followed the crowd into ours, wondering if she could find some of the joy that they had.

She told me she was moved by the worship and the happiness of the people and could feel "what I imagined to be the presence of God." When I gave an invitation that day for those who wanted to receive Christ as Savior, she walked to the front with tears streaming down her face from under her oversized sunglasses.

Almost immediately, she was convinced that what happened to her that Sunday morning would last for a lifetime and would be the answer to her inner longing. Upon inviting Christ into her life, she recalled, she experienced an inner joy and a flood of hope, washing away the heavy despair that she had felt all night long.

Now, she said, *she* had the same joy as the people she had followed into the church. The tears still fell, but now tears of hope and joy were mixed in.

Going back home that day, she could hardly wait until her husband called (knowing that he would). She gladly told him that he should come home, because on Sunday morning she had found the missing piece to the puzzle in her life and in their marriage.

During that week she brought her husband to my study, and I was able to introduce him to Christ. As it turned out, his joy equaled if not surpassed the joy of his newly converted wife.

And it was no flash in the pan. They went on to serve the Lord, together, for many years. Today, over eighteen years later, they are mature believers who walk daily in the joy of the Lord.

CHAPTER 20

CLAUDE UPDIKE AND THE COLONEL

GUATEMALA CITY HAD NEVER seen anything quite like it. Veteran Foursquare missionary Claude Updike was conducting a gospel crusade downtown in Guatemala's teeming capital city. The crusade had drawn thousands and was quickly becoming a spiritual force. Thousands streamed forward to the altar every night to receive Christ as Savior, and the Lord showed Himself present through dramatic miracles of healing and deliverance.

With the whole city buzzing about the impact of the crusade, leaders of the traditional church in Latin America became alarmed and began using all their political power to shut down this upstart evangelical spiritual awakening. Hearing of this new threat, believers who had been praying daily for the revival also began to ask God for protection from those who would hinder the advancement of the gospel in their city. Sure enough, unbeknownst to the missionary and the large, emerging congregation, the president of the country commissioned two platoons of soldiers to disrupt the revival and clearly tell the people, *"No más.* Go home. There will be no more services in the future."

With the aid of the government and its military, Guatemala's "official church" sought to squelch any emergence of evangelical fervor—and particularly any manifestations of the Holy Spirit in such a public meeting.

When the colonel and his soldiers arrived at the service, Pastor Updike was just concluding his message. The colonel, however, felt uncomfortable interrupting the missionary as he was wrapping up his sermon. What would be the harm in waiting until he was done and then making an announcement from the platform?

Besides that, the message was engaging somehow. The soldiers and their leader listened with amazement to the missionary's words. Could these things really be true? Although the colonel didn't realize it at the time, the Holy Spirit was taking the message and bringing strong conviction to his heart. He'd been going through a deeply troubling and unhappy time in his own life and was soon convinced that the sermon that night applied to him and his own situation. When Updike gave the invitation to come forward and receive Christ or be prayed for, the colonel walked to the altar—with a large number of his soldiers following—and embraced Christ as Savior.

The next morning the colonel and some of his officers went to their superior officers and told them not to worry about the services, because they were bringing help and hope and deliverance to some of the most desperate people in the city. Taken aback by this report, the president reconsidered his actions and relented. The crusades could go forward.

As was the practice in Spirit-filled revivals of those days, the new converts were soon trained and put to work as ushers, counselors, and members of prayer teams. Soon the colonel's entire family had come to Christ, and as the services continued night after night, they served the Lord with excitement. Many of the soldiers who had come initially to disrupt and disband the revival ended up taking offerings and praying with fellow citizens who wanted to give their lives to Jesus.

CHAPTER 21

THE HOUND OF HEAVEN

REES HOWELLS WAS A noted nineteenth century Christian who was known as "the Intercessor," since he faithfully prayed for wayward people to come to the Lord.

Howells respectfully referred to the Holy Spirit as the Hound of heaven. He spoke of how God pursues a lost soul through the years, constantly seeking him (or her), wooing him, calling to him. Howell's use of this term was no doubt the inspiration for Francis Thompson's famous poem "The Hound of Heaven."

As the apostle Peter affirmed, "He is patient with you, not wanting anyone to perish, but everyone to come to repentance" (2 Pet. 3:9). The Holy Spirit is not satisfied until He finds the sinner and gives him the opportunity to enter into a relationship with Christ.

> Therefore he is able, once and forever, to save those who come to God through him. He lives forever to intercede with God on their behalf.
> —HEBREWS 7:25, NLT

The transformation of a human life through the salvation and redemption of Jesus Christ is the greatest miracle anyone could imagine—greater than parting the Red Sea, halting the sun and moon in their orbits, or striking down a vast enemy army with a single gesture from an angel.

Yes, the transformation is the miracle. But so is the pursuit! I'd like to illustrate that thought with three short vignettes from my years of ministry.

THE SPIRIT PURSUES THE TOWN DRUNK

Early in my first pastorate I was walking down the hall of our local hospital when I heard a man screaming, cursing, and creating a disturbance so loud that everyone on that wing could hear it. I soon found out that this was the "town drunk" I had read about in the paper. Just a few days earlier, in a drunken stupor, he had wandered into the path of a semitruck rolling into town on a dark and rainy night. The resulting impact had broken almost every bone in the man's body.

On my way out of the hospital I acknowledged two middle-aged women, who turned out to be his daughters. I stopped to say hello, and since I was a pastor, I had to take the brunt of their hatred toward God for allowing their dad to suffer like this.

I quickly made my exit, mumbling that they would be welcome to call me if they needed help. Halfway out to my car, I realized I hadn't even identified myself. I have to confess that the thought brought a smile to my face; maybe I'd inadvertently dodged a bullet!

Somehow, however, the two embittered women managed to track me down, reminding me of my offer to help. The family was apparently exhausted from sitting at this man's bedside day and night (understandably so), and wondered if I would be able to sit with him from seven to eleven o'clock on Friday night.

They caught me off guard. I had given them my word, perfunctorily and insincerely as it may have been offered, and now I had to do it. When I hung up the phone I suddenly remembered that I had a conflict. The high school football game was on Friday night, and several guys from our church played for the home team. Besides that, I was scheduled to give the invocation. Everybody knows that football night is a big deal in Texas, and I'd been looking forward to the game all week. But I had given my word to the two women, so where would I be? Sitting in a hospital room with the reprobate town drunk for the whole evening! All I could do was groan, because there was no way I could get out of my commitment to show up at the hospital.

I took a handful of books with me, hoping to make the best of what I assumed would be a wasted night. When I arrived, Mr. Williams was deeply sedated and was quiet.

The nurse, whose name was Irene and went to our church, asked why I was there. "Why aren't you at the football game?" When I told her how I had been trapped by my own words, she had a big laugh. It gave her the bright idea to tell everyone in the church that I was available to stay with their relatives in the hospital.

At about 9:30 p.m. Mr. Williams came out of his coma-like state and was lucid and calm. He looked at me, wondering who this stranger was, as we had never met before. I told him why I was there, and he thanked me for coming.

At one point, he looked up at me and said, "I don't think I'm going to make it."

"Whether you live or die isn't the issue," I replied. "The issue is, are you prepared to meet God? From what I read in the paper you should have been killed, but God has delayed your death to give you a last chance to get right with Him. Tonight is the time for you to ask for God's forgiveness and put your faith in Christ."

"I've been no good and worthless," he said, "and I have wasted my life. I don't know why God would even care about me. Even if I wanted God, I'm sure He wouldn't want me."

It touched a soft spot in his heart when I told him that I wasn't even supposed to be there that night. I said, "This is the first time I've sat at the hospital for anybody. But I believe God put me here, in His place, to offer you His love and salvation and eternal life. It is important that you repent for wasting your life and that—such as you are—you give yourself to Him. Would you like for me to help you receive Christ?"

"Yes," he said. "Of course!"

After we had prayed, tears flowed down his rugged face—a face that bore all the marks of a hard and wasteful life. The glimmer of a smile appeared. It was obvious to me the Holy Spirit had penetrated his heart. That experience gave me a new appreciation for the song written by the equally wretched John Newton at his conversion: "Amazing grace, how sweet the sound that saved a wretch like me."

Before he went to sleep, he said as we shook hands, "I can't thank you enough for coming." He went to sleep, and fifteen minutes later family members came to take my place.

On my way home my heart overflowed with joy. How good of the Holy Spirit to put me in that place at that time! The next day I returned to the hospital to make some visits, and on my way out I stopped to peek into his room. It was empty. I asked a nurse about Mr. Williams's condition, and she told me he had expired in the night.

That experience had a transforming effect on my value

system. Had I gone to the game that night, I would have soon forgotten who won. But today I am certain that Mr. Williams came to faith in Christ just a couple of hours before he stepped into eternity.

The Hound of heaven had pursued Mr. Williams and overtaken him, and God had given me the privilege of having a front-row seat on the action.

THE SPIRIT PURSUES A SCIENCE PROFESSOR

On the other extreme of the social structure was a man who, at the early stages of the space program, was a top scientist with NASA, in addition to be a longtime science professor at Stanford University. His sister, Carmen, was a member of our church. She had been the coauthor to and secretary of Dr. Ray Jarman, who gained national attention as the pastor of the First Christian Church of South Gate, California, though he was an atheist. (His intention was to socialize and secularize the Scriptures so that people would see the Bible as a book that would help them to understand the lifestyle of good living and peace.)

One night Dr. Jarman attended an informal musical concert of a singer he admired who was a guest in the home of Demos Shakarian, founder of the Full Gospel Businessmen. Oddly enough, Shakarian and Jarman were acquaintances, which paved the way for Jarman to attend this event. During the concert Jarman was so touched by the presence of the Lord and conviction of the Holy Spirit that he fell to his knees and acknowledged the reality of God and Jesus as God's Son. Demos, who was our neighbor and friend, loved to tell about Dr. Jarman's conversion as "the Damascus conversion of Ray Jarman." Soon after Dr. Jarman came to Christ, Carmen had a revelation of the Lord and acknowledged Christ as Savior, turning her life to Christ also.

Carmen and her husband celebrated their fiftieth anniversary in our church fellowship hall. Carmen's brother and his wife, who privately claimed to be atheists, said they would come, but he warned Carmen that she had better not "pull any God stuff on us, or we'll get up and leave."

She let him know that regardless of what he thought about it, this was going to be a Christian celebration. That was all I knew about her brother. I determined it would be best for me to avoid him since he had such an aversion to Christianity.

I came into the event five minutes before it was to start and was soon called to the podium to pray over the festivities. There was no designated seating, so after prayer I looked for my wife and found her sitting at the front round table with one empty seat between her and a distinguished gentleman. I assumed that was where I was to sit. I introduced myself to the man and asked how he knew the Bensons.

When he identified himself as Carmen's brother, I immediately thought he would interpret this as a "Carmen setup" (which was not beyond her).

"Oh," I said, "Carmen told me you are a science professor at Stanford." He smiled politely. Just making small talk, I added, "My nephew Randy played football at Stanford during the John Elway era." I was trying to find a bridge that we could connect with, and I found sports to be the catalyst.

"I enjoy football," he said, "but my game of choice is basketball. I'm a basketball fanatic."

"Did you play?" I asked.

He told me he had played in high school and later at Cal Tech, one of the greatest universities in the world for future scientists. I asked him when he played there, and it was at the same time I played for LIFE Bible College. Probing a little deeper, we found out that we had actually played against one another. (Those guys were brainy but not very athletic; it was comforting to remember that we had beaten them every time we played.)

We had a great conversation, mostly about sports. I did get on him when he admitted to being an Oakland Raiders fan. "I would advise you not to admit that fact to anyone else," I advised him, "because that will diminish your I.Q. by one hundred points." He laughed and jabbed me on the shoulder and came back with some digs. We had connected.

When the event was over, he asked me if we could exchange phone numbers and talk with each other on occasion. He made the first call to me, and we talked several times and became friendly acquaintances. Carmen was thrilled for the new friendship.

One day Carmen told me her brother had a fast-growing cancer and was rapidly failing. The professor's wife, however, wouldn't allow him to have any calls from Carmen or her husband, fearing that they might dare to pray with him or bring up spiritual things.

"Would you please call him, Pastor? He likes you. And if you get through, you can lead him to the Lord."

"Oh, no," I said, "don't put me under that kind of pressure!" I put off making the call as long as possible.

A pastor is always in touch with people who not only want but *expect* you to pray for them. I didn't know how to offer prayer for someone who really didn't want it. And certainly his wife would be on guard against any Christian intruding into their world.

Finally, after lots of prayer and with a great deal of fear and trembling, I made the call. Miraculously, the professor himself answered the phone and seemed elated that I had called. I told him I had been praying for him, and he expressed thanks. Then I mustered the courage to talk to him about the Lord and eternal life. He was very receptive, and I was able to lead him to Christ over the phone.

The Hound of heaven had pursued this one-time atheist to his deathbed and, in spite of his wife's furious opposition, had brought Him to salvation and eternal life.

After he died, Carmen called to tell me that before he passed, her brother asked his wife to give me a piece of moon rock that he had acquired through his work with NASA. Some of the astronauts on their first trip to the moon brought it back with them, and I was honored that he chose to pass such a meaningful souvenir on to me.

THE SPIRIT'S PURSUIT OF A 104-YEAR-OLD WOMAN

An acquaintance of mine, a medical doctor by the name of Cochran, was interviewed to serve as the attending doctor of a hospice. Right off the top he told them, "You probably won't want me, because I'm a Christian. I'd be apt to pray for patients who are physically, spiritually, and emotionally hurting, as well as give them medical attention. Besides that, I'll want to lead them into a personal relationship with Christ if they're not prepared to die."

The members of the board of directors looked at each other,

and one board member spoke for the group: "Not only would we allow you to do that, but we would hope you would do so."

Dr. Cochran speaks with authority on the contrasts of the peaceful death of a person who has a right relationship with God and one who is separated from God, and his experiences are worth hearing.

We in the church never get away from the constant repetition of statistics that say if a person isn't reached for the Lord when they're a child or youth, they will be all but unreachable. Of course, it's certainly our hope to see children make decisions for Christ early in their lives, but I refuse to cede the point that older men and women are unresponsive to the gospel of Jesus Christ. In my years as both a pastor and the president of our denomination, I haven't found that to be the case. In fact, I have met people by the thousands who have committed their lives to Christ in their middle or later years of life.

Dr. Cochran was visiting one of his patients who was a healthy 104 years old. She was exceptionally keen of mind but kept expressing the wish that she could die, because she was "tired of living."

"Are you ready to die?" Dr. Cochran asked her.

The question confused her. "Well," she said, "I'm 104 years old. I guess I'm as ready as a person can be."

"Do you know where you will go after you die?" my friend asked.

She said she had never thought about it. She told him she had grown up in a family where they gave no thought to God. In fact, though she had grown up in the United States, arguably the most Christian nation in the world, she had never heard a presentation of the gospel and asked Dr. Cochran to explain it to her.

When he told her that by trusting in Christ Jesus one could have eternal life, she was very ready to receive the Lord. Dr. Cochran noted that in the next few days there was a marked difference in how this woman viewed her life. She had found a new purpose for living and stopped talking about wanting to die.

It may have taken the Hound of heaven over a century to reach this woman's heart, but reach her He did. And she would spend her last days getting acquainted with the Lord Jesus and anticipating a new life just over the horizon.

It has been amazing to me how the Lord reaches to the lowest level of society or to the highest, and everyone meets at the level ground of the cross of Jesus Christ.

CHAPTER 22

GOD HAS A NEARBY SOLUTION

YEARS AGO MARILEE AND I were visiting the island of
Barbados in the Caribbean. We happened to cross paths
with botany students from a university who were there to do
research. In passing, I asked one of the students about the
nature of their research.

He let us know they were going from island to island studying
various poison berry plants. Their preliminary findings were
that in almost every case where there were poisonous plants,
there would be a plant or a bush that was an antidote within a
few yards. Nature, he explained, had built in a means of coun-
teracting plants that were deadly. I was ready to hear more, but
the students were about to jump on an inter-island express and
head for St. Lucia. I wished that I had the know-how to pursue
the advanced finding of their research.

If this initial finding turns out to have substance, it would be
consistent with the nature of God, because He consistently has
a solution within reach when we find ourselves in trouble. In
Psalm 46:1–2 we read, "God is our refuge and strength, an ever
present help in trouble. Therefore we will not fear." No matter
what the trouble may be, even when our enemies are poised
near at hand, God Himself is also close by.

Call to Me, and I will answer you, and show you great and mighty things, which you do not know.

—JEREMIAH 33:3, NKJV

CHAPTER 23

ANGEL IN A PICKUP

P ETER HOSEIN AND I became friends in 1989 at a Caribbean conference in Puerto Rico under the leadership of missionary Dean Truett. Peter and I and our wives traded lots of visits between Trinidad and Southern California until Peter passed away five years ago. The story of Peter's life is one miracle after another. Peter was an apostolic man of spiritual depth, wisdom, vision, and magnetic personality. I am only seeking to cover three aspects of his life: his conversion, the healing of a severe speech impediment, and a visitation from an angel that saved his life.

UNDERSTANDING THE SCRIPTURE

Peter was a twelve-year-old child of a slave family who had been brought to Trinidad from India. His family was Muslim, and his parents had already dedicated Peter to become a Muslim cleric.

One afternoon after school he went far out of his way to stop at his older brother's general store. He was meandering behind the counter and saw a book that was strange to him. He asked his brother what it was.

"It's a Bible," his brother said.

"What is a Bible?"

"It's a book. It tells about the Christians' God."

"Where did it come from?"

"A poor man came by today and traded his Bible for a dollar's worth of food."

"Can I take it and read it?"

"Yes, if you bring it back."

Peter took the Bible home, not knowing that book, inbreathed by the Holy Spirit, would transform his life and give him experience after experience and opportunities on top of each other. When he got home he began to thumb through its pages, finally settling on the Book of John, since his uncle carried the Muslim name of Ram John. In his simplicity, Peter concluded that this part must be about his uncle, and he might as well begin his reading there.

So he read the Gospel of John, and though it never mentioned his uncle, it gripped his heart in an amazing way. As he read the Gospel, it was as if a light illuminated certain scriptures God wanted him to focus on, and furthermore it was as if he had been given an understanding far beyond his limited twelve-year-old capacity. The Holy Spirit illuminated his young mind to the truth. At the end of the reading he realized—without anyone ever saying a word to him about it or by reading other material—that Jesus was God's Son and that he needed to open his heart and receive Him as Savior. In that moment, he experienced a thorough conversion and never looked back for the rest of his life.

Peter kept on reading and reading the borrowed Bible under the guidance of the Holy Spirit, who had become his Mentor. Concluding that prayer was a needful thing, he created a prayer closet out in the bush behind his house. He established a routine of reading from the Bible and then going out to his place of prayer, away from his family, where he could talk to God about what he had read. (Whom else could he talk to about it?)

After reading in Scripture about Jesus baptizing with the Holy Spirit, he asked the Lord for that experience himself, and one day out in his "closet," he was baptized.

Peter knew of no other Christian in Trinidad. In reading the Scriptures, however, he saw that he needed to be baptized in water, so he went to the local beach and baptized himself.

Over the coming weeks, he carefully shared his new faith with members of his family, who brushed him off, assuming he was "going through a phase." But then something happened that the family could not brush off or ignore. Jesus Himself stepped into Peter's life with an undeniable miracle.

Peter had been born with a terrible speech impediment, barely able to make himself understood sometimes. Rather than encouraging Peter, his cruel schoolteacher deliberately sought to embarrass him, calling him to the front of the class and making him speak—to the mocking laughter of the other children. As you might imagine, this created huge emotional scars upon Peter's self-image. He and his family had accepted the fact that, because of Peter's speech problem, he would always be inferior and a disgrace to the family.

THE UNIQUE HEALING OF HIS SPEECH IMPEDIMENT

Little did Peter know that there were two significant healings on the horizon for him. First, Peter was clearly healed of his shyness and inferiority, becoming a confident young man to the amazement of family and friends who had known him all his life. Could this be the little boy who had been so timid and emotionally stunted? What had come over him? From where had he drawn such confidence and self-assurance? People were constantly asking, "What happened to Peter?" And one day, they would be asking that question with even more amazement and awe.

In the heat of the afternoon, Peter was sitting in his room when Christ Himself appeared to him in a trance or vision. Jesus kindly touched Peter's cheeks and asked him to put out his tongue. As Peter later described it, Jesus had a small stick, something like a popsicle stick. Somehow in this vision Peter could see Jesus from his own vantage point, but he could also see from Jesus' perspective. As Jesus scraped his tongue with the stick, it was as if thousands of tiny worms came off Peter's tongue. This went on for several moments, and each time there were less and less worms.

Finally they were all gone, and his mouth was now clean. Jesus lovingly touched Peter's cheeks and vanished from sight.

Peter had no idea what the vision meant or what the results of that special visitation from the Lord might be. Puzzled, he walked in to the other room to talk to his mother. As he spoke, her eyes suddenly grew very wide.

"Peter!" she cried out. "Your speech impediment is gone!"

Instantly Peter became aware that the heaviness of his tongue had disappeared. From that day on, Peter became a gifted, articulate communicator. As the years would go by, innumerable people would come to Jesus Christ under his spoken ministry.

Later that day, Peter's mother, who had been resistant to Peter becoming a Christian, talked with him and said, "I want to become a Christian." She was the first of many family members and even neighbors who would come to Christ as a result of Peter's miraculous healing. This again would prove the words of the apostle John, "These [miracles] are written that you might believe that Jesus is the Christ, the Son of God, and that by believing you may have life in his name" (John 20:31)

Although still very young, Peter began to teach these new converts all he was learning in the Bible, and they became established in the faith. He took them to the beach and baptized them, and in essence they became Peter's first church. Later he had a group of churches. At this point in his ministry he had never met a Christian who had come to Christ except under his ministry.

All of this had taken place, remember, because of a Bible that had been traded to Peter's brother for a dollar's worth of food.

SAVED BY AN ANGEL

As time went on, Peter felt compelled to conduct public, outdoor services in some of the nearby communities. One night a Muslim woman made the decision to receive Christ as her Savior. When she told her husband of her decision, he was enraged and made the decision to kill Peter.

He knew Peter always traveled by bicycle, and he was aware of the road he took. So one night Peter pedaled his bike down the road, not knowing that a man hid in the bush, crouched at the bottom of a decline in the road, with a sharpened machete, ready to butcher him.

Just as Peter was reaching the crest of the road, a driver in a pickup truck stopped Peter, inviting him to put his bicycle into the bed of the truck and get into the pickup. Surprised, Peter thanked the man for the offer but explained that it wasn't necessary since he was almost home anyway.

The driver then spoke authoritatively: "Put your bicycle into the back, and you get in and ride with me."

Peter did as he was told, frustrating the plans of the man who had been intent on murdering him that night. The driver of the pickup delivered Peter safely to his house, leaving the would-be murderer frustrated in the bush.

It should be noted that Peter, who knew everyone in Trinidad and everything that went on, had never seen that driver and the pickup before, nor did he ever see him since.

The rest of that night and the next day, the Holy Spirit gave the vengeful husband a big dose of conviction for his intentions. The next evening he told his wife he wanted to attend the service with her, and at the end of the service he went forward and put his trust in Christ. He confessed to Peter that the night before he had planned to kill him and asked Peter to forgive him.

For the rest of his life, Peter was an apostolic pastor, preacher, and missionary in the West Indies; but, he also made frequent trips to the U.S., Africa, and Asia. At the very outset of his ministry, however, the Holy Spirit warned him never to become engaged in a battle over the "holy books" of the various religions of Trinidad. It was his job to hold up the Bible, the Word of God, and the Holy Spirit Himself would help people to see the veracity of its claims.

It was a veracity they could see so clearly in Peter Hosein's own life.

CB

About five years ago we visited Trinidad to speak at a convention of the church movement started by Peter. Peter had died, and his absence took a toll on the morale of these people. So I used the occasion to retell many of the stories of how God had used Peter supernaturally through the years, encouraging pastors by letting them know God could equally use them.

At the close of the service, Peter's son and nephew came, bringing an elderly lady to me. They introduced her as the wife of the man who had hidden with a machete in the bush. I asked her if I had told the story correctly. She said, "It was exactly right. It brought back good memories."

CHAPTER 24

A GUERILLA FIGHTER
IS DELIVERED

O N ONE OF OUR visits to Bogotá, Colombia, John and Jean
Firth, our missionary hosts, introduced our group to
Alicia, who gave us her testimony.

She had been totally engaged in the Colombian Civil War,
which had wreaked havoc on the entire country for decades. It
was mostly guerilla warfare, with women as well as men engaged
in savage hand-to-hand combat.

Alicia told us that in the process of the long war and constant
fighting, she had become so calloused and hardened that she
lost all natural human feelings, becoming utterly possessed by
hatred. On the battlefield, she had no fear at all—and no mercy.
Looking back at those days, she concluded that she had so
opened her heart to Satan that she became demon possessed.

She remembered how demons had such control of her that
she felt forced to do outrageous, self-destructive things and
became more like an animal than a human being. On one occasion, an intense morning battle in a forest clearing with two
platoons of the hated enemy had left carnage strewn across the
area. Oblivious to the slaughter, her military company decided
to stay and eat lunch at the battle site. While others sat on the

ground or on stumps, Alicia chose to sit on the chest of one of the slain male enemies .

When she had finished eating, she pulled out a knife from her "war bag" and began casually throwing the blade of the knife into the stomach of the corpse. Then, with the point of her knife, she played a game of tic-tac-toe on the dead soldier's abdomen.

It was nothing to her.

She felt nothing, nothing at all.

She admitted to us that she had become so emotionally numbed by demonic power that she had lost all sense of wrongdoing. What's more, she knew she was possessed, knew she was bound by chains from which she couldn't escape, and didn't care.

Eventually, she was captured, arrested, and thrown into a military prison for life. It was at that prison where Jean Firth first came into contact with Alicia, even obtaining permission to sit in her cell and pray for her. From the very beginning, Jean saw prophetically that Alicia had great potential for the Lord when the demon power would be broken.

Of those demons, Alicia told us, "They kept me wrapped in a cocoon. But deep inside I know I must have cried out to be free."

One day when Jean got too close, Alicia literally recoiled in fear, sensing an impending battle between good and evil. Jean began clapping her hands, saying, "Satan, I am clapping my hands because today Alicia is going to be set free." A voice came from Alicia's mouth—a voice that was not her own. Cowering back from the missionary, the prisoner screamed, "Stop clapping your hands! That sound hurts me."

Jean rejoined, "Devil, I am clapping my hands in praise of the name of Jesus Christ, who is now going to cast you out of Alicia. In the name of Jesus, demons, come out of her!"

Alicia trembled violently—a shaking that lasted for about five minutes as Jean kept insisting on the departure of the demons in Jesus' name. At last, Alicia heaved a great sigh of relief and was completely calm. She had been delivered from Satan's power.

Utterly astounded over Alicia's transformation, the prison guards told the warden she had become a different person since her conversion. Ultimately, the authorities released her to the custody of John and Jean Firth.

Shortly thereafter, Alicia was baptized with the Holy Spirit. As we chatted with her that day in Bogotá, she spoke of the many benefits the Spirit's filling had brought to her life. First, she had sensed a softening in her spirit. Love and compassion, two emotions she hadn't known for years, now flowed through her heart like a living stream.

The Alicia we were seeing and hearing was a completely different person from the cruel-hearted guerilla fighter who had so casually mutilated a Colombian soldier's dead body.

At last report, Alicia was deeply involved in a ministry to women and especially to women in prison.

CHAPTER 25

"YOU'RE LUCKY TO BE ALIVE."

THE BELOVED DR. C. E. Hall was the dean of LIFE Bible College for some twenty years and was a favorite of everyone.

Early in their ministry, Dr. Hall and his wife had been vacationing in their hometown of Canton, Ohio, and were preparing to return to their ministry in Portland, Oregon. Their trip would take them about 2,500 miles and took four days of relatively fast driving over the Rocky Mountains on rough roads that predated the interstate highways.

When they arrived in Portland, Dr. Hall took their car to the dealership to be serviced, which included having the tires rotated. As he was waiting at the dealership, the service supervisor and service mechanic approached him and invited him to come and see his car. They asked him when the last tire rotation took place. Dr. Hall explained that it was done in Canton, Ohio, and that he had driven almost 2,500 miles over the Rocky Mountains days before.

They pointed to the right front wheel, the wheel that bore the most stress. They pointed out that it was obvious the man who rotated the tires fastened the wheel with one lugnut instead of the usual five. All the mechanics were in a state of disbelief as they saw this phenomenon. The general manager of the dealership explained that there was absolutely no way for a car to come that far on those kind of roads without the tire flying off. He observed, "You are lucky to be alive."

Dr. Hall, who would never miss an opportunity like this, responded, "No, it wasn't luck. The Lord was looking out for us."

The manager replied, "That's the biggest miracle I've seen since I've been in the car business."

Dr. Hall quoted Psalm 34:7 to the crowd of salesmen and technicians that had gathered to see the miracle tire: "For the angel of the LORD encamps around those who fear Him."

CHAPTER 26

INNER HEALING FROM THE WORD AND WORSHIP

A CURE FOR PORNOGRAPHY

BEFORE GARY CAME TO Christ, he had accumulated the largest private collection of pornography in the Pacific Northwest.

Indulging in pornography was all that Gary lived for. It had become a fire that burned out everything else in his mind and soul.

But then he met Jesus Christ and invited Him to become the Lord of His life. With the strong help of the Holy Spirit, he immediately got rid of every scrap of the obscene material that had consumed his thoughts and his time for years.

Getting rid of the pornography in his home, however, was one thing. But it was quite a different thing to get the material out of his *mind*. Most of what he had spent his time gazing at was now imprinted indelibly in his memory. It was a stronghold in his mind from which Satan could torment this new believer and seek to make him stumble.

Though Gary knew very well knew he had been forgiven of his past, that his sins had been washed away, and that He was now pronounced righteous through the blood of Christ, the assault on his mind continued day and night.

God, however, was continually patient and gracious to Gary and began to open doors for him to minister to others. He became very effective in his witness and his teaching and eventually pastored a church. But even the demands of full-time ministry didn't diminish the erotic mental images that always seemed to hover in his thoughts.

Then came the day when the Lord spoke into Gary's life that he should become serious about memorizing Scripture—in large portions. So that is what he began to do, starting with the Book of 1 Peter. Accomplishing that, he found the Word to be so strong and powerful in his life that he got the idea of taking on the persona of the apostle Peter and making dramatic presentations to churches and men's group.

He made this presentation one Sunday night at our church, and it made a permanent imprint on many of our people. But the thing that captured my attention was when Gary gave his testimony regarding the unrelenting struggle with pornography.

After a few weeks of memorizing Scriptures, however, Gary one day awakened to the fact that something was different. The crude and vile images that had haunted his thoughts for so many years had faded away. His mind had been washed by the Word.

And he was free.

Gary says that many who have been troubled by dark thoughts of many kinds have heard his testimony and also set about to memorize large portions of Scripture—with the same wonderful results.

> Never underestimate the Scriptures
> And the power that they hold.

They are holy words and healing words,
To cleanse your heart and make you whole.

—Ellen Hagemeyer

Michael Brady

Let me tell you about a friend, Michael Brady. I went to speak at the church where he was the worship leader. I could tell by his leading, singing, and musical ability that he was exceptional.

The next morning the pastor took us for a game of golf, and Michael and I rode the cart together. I asked him about his life. His story needed a context, so he told me how in his childhood it was discovered that he and his older brother had a love and talent for music. When they reached their high school years they were enrolled in a parochial school that focused on music. It was an education of the highest quality. But the benefits came at a serious cost in that some of the instructors and clergy were sexually abusive, which left Michael with emotional scarring.

After high school Michael sang in the well-known Mitchell Boys Choir of California. While still a teenager he and his brother and another friend formed musical group called the Sandpipers. They became very famous for songs like "Guantanamera," which was a hit the world over; "Come Saturday Morning;" and "The Wonder of You." After traveling the world in concert, the schedule took its toll on any kind of normalcy in their lives, and they disbanded the group.

Michael then began working as a studio musician, playing for many popular recording stars. I found out, separate from Michael, that he was such a gifted musician that he was in great demand.

During our conversation, I asked him how he came to meet

the Lord. It seemed to start when he was married. His wife wanted to begin attending church, so on this one Sunday, as a favor, he went to church with her to get her initiated. The pastor was pleased that they were going to start going to church. However, Michael made it a point to let the pastor know his wife would come, but he played golf on Sundays.

Somehow the pastor found out about Michael's musical background, so several weeks went by before the pastor called Mike to ask for his help. The bass guitar player in the church's outstanding worship team was going to be out for several Sundays, and the pastor asked Michael to fill in for a few weeks. Because Michael remembered the favorable impression he had toward the worship part of the service, he told the pastor he would come. He enjoyed singing as well as playing the guitar. He started singing the worship songs. These praises to the Lord resonated in his heart and became a part of his being.

Remember the abuse he suffered at the hands of some of the teachers in high school, which left painful memories and scars he thought he would have to live with the rest of his life? One Sunday a surprising awareness came to him—all of those inner scars had been healed, and he had became a new man, never again showing a trace of the old life that had tormented him.

Once again the truth of Scripture had manifested: "If the Son therefore shall make you free, ye shall be free indeed" (John 8:36, KJV).

Never Underestimate the Cleansing Power of Worship

Today, Mike is the worship leader of a church the San Fernando Valley, and his brother is also a born-again believer and a worship leader in his own church. Michael gave up Sunday golf for the Lord but now plays with his friends at a country club during the week. God is good!

CHAPTER 27

MISTAKES ON PURPOSE

DR. KELLEHER

D R. KELLEHER, YOU MUST go to Customer Service."
Dr. Bob Kelleher, a council member in our church, and his wife, Janet, had gone to the Nordstrom department store to buy Bob a couple of suits. When it came time to pay, the sales associate told Bob that there seemed to be a problem with his account and that it would be necessary for him to talk to someone in the customer service department.

Dr. Bob and his wife were shocked. *A problem with the account?* After all those years of being loyal customers? What in the world could that mean? For generations, Nordstrom has maintained a well-deserved reputation for treating their customers with the highest degree of courtesy and respect, so how could something like this happen?

The doctor was so angry to have to go and stand in line in the credit department that he started to take out his frustrations on his wife. Had *she* been making too many purchases? Overcharging their card? He almost felt like storming back to the men's department and telling them they could keep their suits.

"Just calm down," Janet told him. "It's probably just a misunderstanding. It'll be worth the time we've spent today. You'll see."

So as Dr. and Mrs. Kelleher found themselves waiting in a

rather long line of credit customers, his eye was drawn to the lady in a sleeveless sundress standing just in front of them.

With a physician's keen eye, Dr. Kelleher knew immediately that the mole located on back of the woman's shoulder, in a place where she would probably never notice, was most likely cancerous. It wasn't just a wild guess. Dr. Kelleher had been a practicing oncologist but later changed his specialty to plastic surgery, primarily to help correct unsightly scars created by cancer. As a result, the lady in the credit line with a dangerous mole couldn't have found a more skilled and practiced eye than the one that belonged to the man standing immediately behind her.

Stepping back a bit, Bob made quiet comments to his wife that the mole didn't look good. But should he say anything? Would she be offended? Maybe he should just mind his own business.

Janet put it into perspective when she asked him, "If you were her, what would *you* want a doctor to do?"

"I would want him or her to tell me," he replied. "Immediately!"

After a bit of a discussion, they concluded that as Christians, they were truly "their sister's keeper." Besides, they were both by nature gregarious, caring people.

As quietly and cordially as they knew how, they invited the lady out of the credit line and asked her to step out into the empty hallway with them. Dr. Kelleher identified himself as a medical doctor and a surgeon and told her what he had seen on her shoulder, suggesting she have the mole diagnosed immediately.

You never know how someone will take news like that—particularly from a stranger—but this woman was gracious and grateful. She took down their names so she could let them know what happened.

To jump forward in the story, after tests were taken, Dr. Kelleher's concerns were completely justified. The mole was indeed malignant and already sending roots deep into the woman's shoulder muscle. As the surgeons sought to excise the entire melanoma, it miraculously came out in its entirety—which seldom happens in such surgeries.

Dr. Bob and Janet received a card from the woman, who had been completely delivered from the cancer and was profuse in her thanks.

To return to that day in the credit department at Nordstrom, Dr. Kelleher's attitude changed after he was able to help the lady with the mole. Maybe there was a reason for his standing in that line after all. When his turn came with the accounts representative, the clerk apologized for what must have been a mistake. There was no issue with the Kellehers' credit at all. The misunderstanding should never have happened.

Bob and Janet, however, knew better. God had placed them in the right place at the precise time to help a woman in need—who didn't even know she was in need.

What had seemed like an irritating inconvenience in the course of life turned into an opportunity to save a life.

THE HAWAII SURFER

On the beautiful islands of Hawaii an inordinate number of youth spend a lot of time surfing. It is a surfer's paradise and a beautiful thing to watch them ride the waves. It seems like such a pleasant sport, but surfing has quite a few inherent dangers; such as being attacked by a shark, drowning, or in this case, getting cut by the fin of a surfboard.

On this day twelve-year-old Kyle Watson was surfing with his youth pastor, who went by the name of Tom-Tom. Though Kyle was known to be an excellent surfer, his surfboard flipped on him, and the sharp fin cut a huge eight-by-eight–inch gash on the upper inside of his leg. It was such a big slash that their first thought was that he had been bitten by a shark. Tom-Tom could clearly see that the wound was all the way to the bone.

Kyle was in real trouble, losing blood and showing obvious signs of going into shock. The youth pastor had to act fast. Quick and right decisions were imperative to save Kyle's life. There was only time for the profound prayer, "Lord help us!"

And help the Lord did. Tom-Tom raced to a house near the beach and quickly told the lady about Kyle's accident. He asked if she would call the paramedics. Yes, she would, she told him, and immediately identified herself as a registered nurse who worked in a trauma center.

She came running to Kyle's side, letting him know the paramedics were on their way. She analyzed the wound and found that though there was a lot of bleeding, the artery was not severed. Kyle was going into shock, but she was able to stabilize him and get him ready for the paramedics, who were by then arriving. To Kyle and Tom-Tom, this nurse on the beach was a godsend.

The paramedics rushed Kyle to the hospital, but there seemed to be a mistake. It was assumed they would take him to Castle Hospital, which was only five miles away, but instead they transported him to The Queen's Hospital, which was at least twice the distance. It seemed something had gone wrong.

As the medical team was preparing for surgery, the lead surgeon came out and introduced himself. He gave an encouraging prognosis as to the possible success of the procedure.

It so happened that the heart surgeon, who had a reputation as the best on the islands, happened to be in that hospital that day. He never practiced at either the Castle or The Queen's hospitals, but that day he was at Queen's to perform a delicate heart procedure for a friend. Just as he was completing that surgery, the trauma doctors asked him to examine the extent of Kyle's injury. He confirmed the main artery was not severed but was badly damaged. He suggested that since heart surgeons are especially skilled with respect to arteries, this procedure should be done by a heart surgeon. He volunteered, since he was there, to stay and do the procedure if it was OK with the boy's family.

The family answered rhetorically, "OK? Yes! Yes! Yes!" They saw this as an extraordinary occurrence orchestrated by the Lord. Now Kyle's loved ones understood why the paramedics went to The Queen's Hospital, which to them seemed the *wrong* hospital in this moment of emergency, to have the surgery by the *right* doctor.

The procedure was so successful and the healing process was so efficient that Kyle was back in the surf in ten weeks.

ⓒЗ

The message of Dr. Kelleher's and Kyle's experiences show that God doesn't always protect us from the accidents or irritants of life—the lion's dens or fiery furnaces or storms—but He is watching and working. As promised by Scripture, God is working things for our good. (See Romans 8:28.) I remind myself when things go wrong not to get so bent out of shape that I become blinded to the wonderful workings of God.

CHAPTER 28

INSIDER INFORMATION

I include this story as a reminder that one can rely on the Lord in all areas of life. Additionally, it cannot be stressed enough that God is interested in everything that concerns you: job, finances, vacations, relationships of all kind, marriage, health, and everything else you can think of.

ABOUT FIVE YEARS AGO, Marilee and I began to pick up on big signs and loud warnings that the bottom was about to fall out of the Southern California real estate market. We wanted to sell our house before anything like that happened, but we also needed top dollar—the house's highest prevailing price.

I asked a number of my friends in real estate when they thought the market would actually peak, but they didn't want to commit themselves. "It would just be a guess or pure conjecture," they told me.

Even my son Mike, the L.A. County president of Chicago Title Company, would only say, "Only God knows."

I felt like saying, "Thanks, Mike. I know that *He* knows. I want to know what *you* know."

One time he looked at me and said, "Why don't you put out a fleece?"

A fleece. Well, I'd heard that before. Mike loves fleeces.

When he was in high school, his mother taught him the story about Gideon's fleece. Gideon was so afraid about a divine directive, but the fleeces turned him into a "mighty man of valor." (See Judges 6–7.) Mike loved that story and has practiced it at various crossroads in the course of his life—including major business decisions. He even tells some of his non-Christian colleagues and employees about Gideon fleeces. At our house we refer this as Mike's fleece rather than Gideon's fleece.

So that's the advice he gave me—when I was looking for something a little more tangible and specific.

"What kind of fleece would you make in a circumstance like this?" I asked him.

He suggested that we ask that when the market reached its peak, the Lord would send someone by to knock on our door and let us know they wanted to buy our house.

I countered his suggestion by saying that could never happen.

His answer was, "That's why it is such a good fleece. You don't make them easy, but you make them hard so you clearly know the answer is from God."

I thought, "Why am I, the pastor, getting a lecture from my businessman son?"

I admit that I had almost forgotten our conversation until the doorbell rang fifteen days after our prayer. The man identified himself as a neighbor, called me by name, and told me his purpose. "I'm here to ask if would be willing to sell your house. This is my wife's dream house, and she asked me to buy it for her."

Immediately, I conjured up the most apathetic countenance I could imagine. "Hmmm," I said. "Well, I don't know. I'll talk to my wife and see what she says. If you want to come back in three days, we can talk."

He did come back, and for the next three weeks we did some heavy-duty negotiations before we came up with a price to settle on.

Months later, a real estate friend told me that the sale took place in the vicinity of time between when the market was reaching the peak and before it suffered its catastrophic drop.

It is remarkable to see the wide range of help God gives us in the abundant scope of His workings. He will show you when to stop and when to go.

In Psalm 103:2, which as been dubbed as "David's Hallelujah Chorus," he seems to raise his voice in praise as he considers the *advantages* godly people have through their relationship with the Lord. "Bless the LORD, O my soul, and forget not all his benefits [advantages]" (KJV).

Chapter 29

"God Sent You."
"No, Not Really."

A twenty-year-old woman who had visited our church came with quite a story.

She had grown up in an affluent suburban home, but in her last two years of high school—and against her parents will and desires—she began going with a young man who lived on the wild side.

Just as her parents had feared, he had a terrible influence on their daughter. Over time, she defied all the principles her parents had instilled in her and began living a promiscuous lifestyle with him. At first her parents tried to reason with her, but to no effect. Finally, because they had reached an impasse and her dad didn't know what else to do, he threatened to disown her if she didn't stop going with him. She retaliated by moving in with the guy, who was known to be an unscrupulous young man.

The sad story developed from there, as so many such stories have progressed. She had two children out of wedlock, and the young man turned out to be as cruel, hateful, and abusive as everyone thought he would be. He beat her both physically and verbally, and the little ones as well.

When she finally left that evil young man, her parents pleaded with her to come home, but her pride wouldn't allow it. Instead, she determined to make it on her own, because "I don't need anybody to help me." She moved into a house in one of the worst sections of town.

Then came a night that was very, very dark. She felt that she was tormented by Satan himself. Hadn't she ruined her own life and the life of her children? What was the use of going on? How could a life this badly damaged ever be repaired?

From her Sunday school classes as a child, she remembered the story of the prodigal son, whose life sank to the very bottom before he eventually found his way home to his father. But how could she ever go home? She had wandered too far, and she could never bring herself to ask for forgiveness.

After a restless Friday night, on Saturday morning she had come to the conclusion that she was so void of hope she might as well end it all, destroying both her life and that of the children as well.

First, however, she would tell the Lord what she had in mind. If He didn't somehow intervene, she would turn on the gas, open the oven door, and end their misery.

She said, "I will wait about fifteen minutes, Lord, and if You are aware of me and care about me, have someone get in touch with me in some way, maybe come by or call."

That morning I had gone to visit a family who lived the upscale part of town. As I was returning to the church, I took an unlikely route down a particular street rather than a main thoroughfare through the town. It happened to be a street with no stop signs, and I knew I could drive faster and get back to the church more quickly.

It never occurred to me that the single lady with two little ones lived on that street, and I sped by her house without a second thought. I was almost at the end of her block when a picture of her face flashed in my mind, and I thought to myself, "This is the street where that girl lives—the one who messed up her life, the one who visited our church once. I wonder if she still lives in that shanty? I'll just knock on her door and invite her back to church."

I braked the car hard, threw it into reverse, and backed up for about a full block to her house. My expectations for the impromptu visit were so minimal that I even left the car running. Surely this would only take a moment.

I knocked and heard a stirring inside, but no one came to the door.

I knocked once again, asking myself if I had come by too early on Saturday morning. I was going to give it another minute or so, and if she didn't answer, I'd just jump back into the car and go.

But she did answer. The door swung open, and when the young lady saw me her eyes went very wide. She almost yelled, "God sent you!"

My first thought was, "No, God didn't send me. I just happened by on my way back to the church." But I didn't say anything and just waited for a little enlightenment.

She quickly told me her story, concluding that she had been about five minutes away from killing herself and her children.

We talked and prayed together that the Lord would wash her life clean, forgive her of all her sins, and help her to experience a new beginning. I assured her that God had a beautiful purpose—even now—for her life and for each of her little ones. Because she had turned to Him, He would once again restore hope in her heart and give her a future. She responded with great sincerity.

I asked her to take her children and go home to her father and mother and, like the prodigal son, ask for forgiveness with a contrite heart. That's just what she did, and to her parents' credit, they received her with arms as wide open as the father in Jesus' story. It was truly a great reunion and reconciliation.

The next day, Sunday, she was in church with her children, eager for her new beginning. And I can vouch that it was the start of great new life. The Bible teaches us in Romans 8:28 that bad things can and will happen, but the amazing thing is that God works on those things. If we turn to Him, He has the power and wisdom to turn them to good.

CHAPTER 30

FOUR MORE YEARS

I DA CARR AND HER son Tim came to Florence Avenue in 1974. When I became acquainted with her, she had cancer of the tongue and face, and it was spreading. Things looked pretty bleak.

Ida's surgeon was Dr. Sid Ellery, a noted oncologist. When he sat down with Ida in his office, he didn't pull any punches with her. The surgery would require the removal of her tongue, with a good chance that part of her cheek would also be involved, if the cancer had spread into her face. Ida had to be wondering just what she would look like—and what life would be like—when she came out of anesthesia. There was no guarantee she would even survive the surgery.

As we talked, it was obvious that the disease was already taking a physical and emotional toll on our new friend. She had lost thirty pounds in one month and seemed to be failing fast.

A single mother with one son in the Air Force and another fourteen-year-old still at home, Ida was tormented with the thought of leaving her youngest alone in the world with nowhere to go. She *had* to find a way to live through it!

As arrangements were made for the procedure, she and Dr. Ellery had a heart-to-heart talk. No, she certainly didn't want to die, but greater than her fear of death was her fear of leaving young Tim to fend for himself. She repeatedly explained that to the doctor, probably hoping he could do something miraculous to just give her four more years of life.

That was all she asked. Just four more years. Tim would be eighteen by then, and capable of moving on into life without her.

Dr. Ellery assured her they would do everything medically they could, but there were no guarantees. When Ida worried out loud about her young son being burdened with funeral arrangements, the doctor suggested that between then and the surgery she needed to get some of those concerns out of her mind. She needed to be as stress-free as possible to give post-surgical healing a chance.

As a result, she went to the Norwalk Funeral Home, where she picked out her casket and made arrangements to cover all the bills.

Just recently, as I was writing her story, she reminded me of a detail I had forgotten. Two weeks before her scheduled surgery, we had a Sunday night service at our church where the emphasis was on healing. She explained that because she had lost so much weight she was embarrassed that her clothes no longer fit her properly, so she made it a habit to sit in the back row.

As the service concluded, I asked people who needed healing to stand for prayer and then called on the people sitting close to them to also stand and pray for them. Ida reminded me that while the congregation prayed, she felt a strong, warm hand on her back.

Then, remembering that she was seated in the back row, she turned around to see who it was, but there was no one there. "It had to be the Lord," she told me later.

From then on, much of Ida's fear over the future melted away. I should mention that Ida and her son had just come to the Lord a few weeks prior to visiting our church, so praying for healing was new to her—as were experiencing the presence of God and miracles.

The night before the surgery, I visited her at Long Beach Memorial Hospital. When I walked into her room, I found her calm and smiling. She had done all she knew to ready herself, and she had left the outcome of the surgery and her future in the hands of God.

"Ida," I told her, "the whole church is praying for you. We're praying that your condition won't be as serious as the doctors have said, and that the surgery won't have to be extensive. We're also praying that you'll have a longer life than you can imagine."

Before I prayed again with her, she stopped me. In a quiet and respectful way, she reminded me of her desire. All that she was asking God for was *four more years* of life.

Ida had understandably reasoned that because of the magnitude of her deteriorating cancerous condition and the low expectations of the surgeons four more years would be miracle enough!

I went back to see Ida the next afternoon following the surgery, and Dr. Ellery happened to be there. He was all smiles. He explained that they had found Ida's situation much better than expected. All the tests they had run prior to surgery indicated something very ominous. The team had gone into surgery expecting to removed Ida's tongue and much of her cheek tissue, which would have seriously compromised her ability to swallow—and of course, to speak.

Instead, they only had to remove the nickel-sized tumor from her tongue. The surrounding tissue was clean.

Smiling again as he left, he told Ida, "Again, I won't guarantee it, but right now it looks very favorable to me that you'll get your four more years!"

ℭℬ

Ida is still living, thirty-five years after the surgery in 1974. At the time of the surgery she was thirty-nine years old, and of course you remember her son Tim was fourteen. At the time of this writing, Ida is seventy-three and Tim is forty-nine and a lieutenant in the Los Angeles County Sherrif's Department. He has been married fifteen years to a great wife, and they've given Ida two granddaughters.

Four more years of life?

Yes—and then some!

Every time I see Ida, I'm reminded of Ephesians 3:20: "Now all glory to God, who is able, through his mighty power at work within us, to accomplish infinitely more than we might ask or think" (NLT).

It also reminds me that my chief failure in prayer has not been that I ask too much but rather that I expect too little.

CHAPTER 31

YOU MADE MY LIFE

I AWOKE IN THE NIGHT with a face imprinted so very clearly on my mind.

It was the face of Mary Jayne May.

It all started, I suppose, in my evening prayer time, when I had asked the Holy Spirit to bring to the forefront of my mind anything I needed to do with regard to hurting people in our denomination.

It was a relief to me when nothing came to mind. I closed my Bible and went to bed.

But, at about 2:00 a.m. I was suddenly wide awake—with Mary Jayne May's face clearly in my mind's eye. The Holy Spirit gave me a picture of her in vivid, three-dimensional, living color, and it was no mystery why He did so. I had asked Him to reveal unresolved issues in my life, and that's exactly what He was doing.

I knew I had wronged Mary Jayne May.

The whole story flashed before my eyes, probably in an instant, but I lived it for the rest of the night. I had been part of a group that had been neither kind nor just with this dear woman. In fact, I had personally wronged her through my cowardly silence when I ought to have spoken up.

All the details of the incident came flooding back into my

mind, along with a big dose of conviction in my heart. I had always been somewhat dubious that one individual could ask God to forgive a corporate group, but on that night I asked anyway. I confessed for all of us and admitted before the Lord that I had been as wrong as anyone, because I didn't stand when I should have and could have made a difference. I had been unwilling to risk the disapproval of influential friends who had lined up in opposition against her. And though the incident was now many years in the past, it made me feel ashamed all over again.

Mary had been part of a two-woman pastoral team, unusual perhaps, even for our denomination, which seeks to encourage women in ministry. These were ladies who had team-pastored for decades, had proven themselves competent and effective over the long haul, and had brought good will and glory to the Lord in their place of ministry. These were good and godly women, and they had poured their lives and resources into the mid-sized church they pastored. They had served faithfully, loyal to their flock and loyal to the denomination.

The women had enjoyed wide acceptance in their city until a situation developed that was unlike anything I had ever seen before. Almost overnight it seemed, a large group of detractors came on the horizon, seeking to take over this particular church and remove the two lady pastors. In hindsight, this was a group that should never have been accepted as part of our denominational family. I don't have time or space to give details as to how evil and un-Christlike they were, nor as to the reproach they brought to our denomination and to the kingdom of God.

Now here I was, years later, losing sleep as I thought about how our denominational leadership had handled that situation—and the part I had played in our decisions. I could hear the Lord's voice clearly say to me, "Why did you stand in quietness and not stand with this lady as she was crucified alone?"

I didn't have an answer.

There's nothing like hindsight, is there? Looking back now, I can see this group for what it truly was: bitter; crude; and heartless to any individual, pastor, or church that was not of their ilk. But they had deceived some of our leadership, including some of our best and most conscientious.

And then there were people like me, who probably knew better but didn't want to make waves.

Let me just quickly summarize by saying there was a denominational meeting to resolve the tense situation in the church where these ladies pastored, and our leadership sided with the group that sought to take over that church. As a result, the women were compelled to give up their pastorate.

When push came to shove, I took the easy road of consensus and let the women stand alone. The leaders of the rebel group walked away dusting off their hands, as if to say their unrighteous victory had been a stamp of approval of their character. A little later, one of the woman pastors went to be with the Lord, leaving her ministry partner to bear this rejection alone.

But why would the Lord have brought these things to my mind if He hadn't intended to give me a chance to make things right? By 4:00 a.m. I had already formulated my plan of action and the tenor of my apology, and I could hardly wait for daylight. With deep longing in my heart, I asked the Lord for courage and wisdom to take responsibility and to ask for forgiveness.

I drove in to the office that morning gripped with a sense of determination. When I arrived at work, I called Cheryl, one of the four women who worked with me, to see if we could find this former pastor. I had chosen that particular woman because she was a former missionary and more familiar with the denomination network.

When I mentioned Mary Jayne's name, Cheryl smiled. "Yes, I can find her," she said. "She's my mother's best friend. They're together every day, and I can have her on the phone in five minutes." What an indicator that God had gone before me!

I let Mary Jayne know that I had stayed awake most of the night thinking about the wrong our denominational family had done to her. But more than that, I confessed that I too had done her wrong, because I hadn't been willing to stand up for her when I had plenty of influence to do so.

"I feel so ashamed," I told her. "I don't think I have the right, in any way, to be considered Christlike. I called to ask you to forgive me, if you have it in your heart."

Mary Jayne didn't even hesitate. "Of course I forgive you," she said. She went on to say that she and her team-pastor, Louise, had loved our church family, and as far as she was concerned, nothing would ever change that. "We knew we had been terribly wronged," she went on, "but we never felt that was the intention of the denomination as a whole but rather of just a few individuals."

I asked her if she would come to our headquarters in Los Angeles so we could publicly apologize to her and restore them to the church—Mary Jayne, in person, and Louise, posthumously. I told her we also wanted to make up for some of the financial losses they had suffered as a result of our actions at that time.

It was a great moment for me when Mary Jayne graciously accepted our offer and agreed to come.

As we were wrapping up our conversation, there was a few seconds' lapse. I could sense she still had something to say.

"Paul," she finally said. "Paul, you have made my day. Or maybe it would be more correct if I told you, you have made my *life*."

The day we had Mary Jayne return to the church family turned out to be one of the most satisfying days of my denominational leadership. I never could have imagined that making it right with an elderly trooper would be so fulfilling.

It had a miraculous effect on Mary Jayne, and even more so on me!

CHAPTER 32

DR. MITZNER, THE
MAN OF PRAYER

EVERYONE KNEW THAT IF Dr. Herman Mitzner prayed for you, something was going to happen. He taught that 1 Thessalonians 5:17—"Pray without ceasing" (KJV)—didn't mean to be in prayer every moment of the day. It rather meant that once you start praying for something, don't stop until the answer comes!

This great man was often in our home when I was a youngster. He and my dad, both from German immigrant families, were fast friends and always enjoyed being together.

At our dinner table, I remember him telling story after story of great and miraculous answers to prayer that he had witnessed. What impressed me most was the way he spoke about God—as if, like Moses, he knew the Lord as a close friend.

I personally observed the miracle in the following story, watching it all from a "catbird seat" in an upper bunk. And though I was only eleven years old at the time, I still remember it in great detail. I had opportunity through the years that followed to verify the story in many ways, as you will see.

As I grew into adulthood my conviction has been that he was one of those individuals who was not only a man of prayer but was additionally one of the rare people who had the gift of miracles, which would account for the exceptional manifestation of miracles. A credit to Dr. Mitzner was that with his success in supernatural results, he never needed or wanted the limelight. He was content pray for a broken foot out of the public eye or in the back room of a church or through prayer cloths sent back and forth to the mission field by envelopes.

CLYDE GREISEN

The Christian youth camp was located on a beautiful lake in Wisconsin. Sports and swimming were the highlights of the camp, and as far as I was concerned it couldn't get much better. After spending at least two hours in the lake, I joined the crowd that had gathered at the baseball diamond to watch a softball game between the youth all-stars and the pastors.

Both teams were good, and the competition was fierce. As I remember, the pastors had more pride than skills and probably weren't nearly as good as they remembered themselves being. As a result, they played with an attitude, hoping to make up for their deteriorating athletic skills with sheer determination.

But I do recall being impressed with the athletic ability of Pastor Clyde Greisen, a highly respected and loved pastor whose life touched thousands as a pastor and Bible college professor. Here was a man who truly understood the game and played smart.

After hitting a solid single and approaching first base, he determined to dig in and make the attempt to reach second. He knew he'd have to slide into the base, which he did skillfully—but then suddenly collapsed in agonizing pain on the field.

Apparently, he hadn't realized that the rustic camp baseball field had large rocks just under the dirt. A cleat on his right baseball shoe caught on a rock, and he fell, hard, somehow shattering bones in his ankle and foot. Blood spurted, soaking his socks, shoes, and pants. Bones from multiple compound fractures literally protruded through his skin.

Someone ran to call an ambulance.

Suddenly, in the middle of the excitement, Dr. Mitzner strode onto the field and took charge.

No one was much surprised by his first directive: "Cancel the ambulance!" After assessing the situation, he said, "Let's take him into this first dorm, lay him on a cot, and pray for his healing."

I'd like to make three quick notes at this point in the story. First, the dorm to which they took Dr. Greisen happened to be my dorm. That gave me the opportunity to be there and observe firsthand everything that followed.

Second, in the last ten years of his life, Dr. Greisen became the minister to seniors at our Florence Avenue church. He and I often discussed the incident in minute detail, recalling together his point of view, writhing in pain, and my perspective as a wide-eyed little kid watching the proceedings from my upper bunk in my dorm.

Third, this was an accident that predated orthopedic surgeries as we know them today, where they can use screws, bolts, rods, pins, and high technology to mend shattered bones. Dr. Mitzner would have known very well that if God chose not to perform a miracle in that youth camp dorm, Dr. Greisen would have been lame the rest of his life.

If Mitzner had any doubt about a forthcoming miracle, it certainly wasn't obvious to any of us in the room that day. "This is going to be a great opportunity for God to receive glory when Clyde is healed," he said. In that dire and gloomy setting, Mitzner was already presuming a miracle with unwarranted boldness. He was acting and talking like something great was about to happen, and he wasn't going be denied. I hasten to add here that his attitude didn't have the slightest whiff of cockiness or self-confidence; it was obvious to all of us that he wholly trusted the Lord.

As he prayed over the injured pastor, Mitzner kept reminding God of His promises. Of course, I can't remember the specific Scriptures he quoted that day, but it went something like this: "Lord Jesus, You say in John 14:13, 'Whatsoever ye shall ask in my name, that will I do, that the father may be glorified in the Son.' So Lord, we ask in the name of Jesus that you heal Clyde's ankle and foot and make it perfectly well. Now, we know You are faithful to Your Word, and You would not make those promises unless You intended to keep them." And so it went, with many such verses.

Finally, Mitzner asked the pastors to help Greisen onto the floor to stand on his left foot. He then directed Greisen to put his fractured foot on the floor.

When his foot touched the floor, the injured man passed out.

At that point, several pastors expressed their displeasure and said, "Let's call the ambulance and take him to the hospital."

Dr. Mitzner, however, wouldn't hear of it. "No, no," he said. "We can't quit now, because I *know* God is going to heal him."

In our years together at Florence Avenue, I told Dr. Greisen how bad I'd felt for him that day when he passed out. I think I came down on the side of the pastors who wanted to call the ambulance. Dr. Greisen admitted candidly, forty-five years after the event, that when Mitzner wanted to continue praying, "I hurt so bad that I could have choked him."

Mitzner began another round of prayer, claiming yet more of the prayer promises in Scripture. (And believe me, he could quote them all.)

"Stand him up!" he directed. He felt that with prayer there should also be a corresponding step of faith. So they stood Greisen up, and he fainted again. More pastors left in disgust, almost in rebellion. Greisen himself, in his great agony, was furious and wanted to go the hospital.

Mitzner, however, was oblivious to them all. He asked for one more round of prayer, adding, "I believe this is the time." And yet again he began praying the promises of God from the pages of the Scriptures.

"Let's stand him up again," he said.

This time, as Greisen's foot touched the cement floor, something snapped in the injured foot and ankle. Daring greatly, he put his full weight on the foot, and there was no pain. We could all see—though we could hardly believe what our eyes were seeing—that there were no more protruding bones and that the foot was whole.

Griesen began walking around the room, his anger turned to wonder, recognizing that he had experienced an incredible miracle. And one of the things I remember most vividly from the event was how he hugged Mitzner, holding on to him like he would never let him go.

The few pastors who were left in the room took him by car to the camp infirmary, where the RN medicated the gashes against infections, wrapped the foot and ankle, and told him to get to a doctor for precautionary measures when he returned home to Urbana, Illinois. Because there was no swelling, his foot fit perfectly back into his shoe. He walked to the dining hall that evening without so much as a limp, and the many who had seen the accident were stunned. Some of the pastors who had walked away from the scene of the miracle in anger and disgust looked more than a little sheepish.

The next morning, Saturday, Dr. Greisen left the camp for home in Urbana. With his two young teenagers in the car, he took the wheel himself, driving over three hundred miles and using his right foot to operate the gas pedal and brake.

He preached twice on the following Sunday. On Monday morning, his wife insisted that he go to the doctor. He told the doctor he needed an x-ray of the foot he had broken and wanted to see how it was healing. Examining the x-rays some time later, the doctor exclaimed, "You had some nasty breaks, but whoever set the bones did an incredible job. It's all healing up fine. My, it almost looks like a miracle to me."

In later years, Dr. Greisen admitted that he wouldn't have even been able to remember which foot had been injured, if not for the memory of being forced to use it on the long drive home. Neither the ankle nor the foot ever bothered him again.

A MOTHER'S PROMISE

Virginia Smith Fromm is the older sister of Chuck Smith, founding pastor of Calvary Chapel Costa Mesa and the father of the Calvary Chapel movement around the world. In the following account, she tells the story of her miraculous healing as a two-year-old girl. The miracle occurred only a few short months before Chuck's birth.

My family was what you might call a "church-oriented family"—good people but not living whole-heartedly for the Lord. My father, Charles, was an elder and Sunday school superintendent in our church, as well as a Boy Scout leader and an active member in the sheriff's reserve.

In later years, I came to understand that his non-stop busyness was a way of dealing with an inner emptiness; he was searching for something to fill that void in his heart. When I was nine years old, however, my mother, Maude, began looking for help and wandered into a tent revival. The evangelist was Aimee Semple McPherson. At the close of the meeting my mother gave her heart to Jesus, which filled the vacuum in her heart.

My mother's conversion experience so disturbed my father that he tried to close the tent meeting down. In the process of meeting with the organizers of the revival meeting, however, he too found the reality of a living Christ.

At about that time I became violently ill. My cousin had died of spinal meningitis just a week before. When I went into convulsions, my mother was sure I was dying. A nurse living in the same building told my her, "Get that child to a doctor immediately!"

My mother told her, "Jesus is going to heal my baby."

Instead of taking me to a doctor, she ran next door with me to the church parsonage. Herman Mitzner, a young evangelist at the time, was staying with the pastor while holding meetings at the church. The two men were walking out of the house to go to the evening service when mother stopped them in a panic and told them that her daughter was dying. Dr. Mitzner told the pastor to go on to the service, and he would stay and pray for the little girl.

They laid me on a bed, and by this time my eyes had rolled back in my head. My spine had gone limp, and my head was touching my feet. I had the death rattle in my throat and had stopped breathing.

I was gone.

Dr. Mitzner had my mom and grandmother go into a corner of the room and pray. He told them to get their eyes off of me and on to Jesus.

Dropping to her knees, my mother prayed: "Oh Lord, I know You are able to do anything. You are able to give my child back to me, restored in health. If you heal my child, I will rededicate my life to You for whatever ministry You might have for me and my unborn child." (My mother was carrying another baby at the time.)

My dad rushed into the room and was told that I had died. "If you want to see her alive again," Dr. Mitzner told him, "go to the corner of the room and pray for her." He dropped to his knees and began pleading for God to heal me.

And that is just what He did.

I began to breathe again, my body straightened out, and I called out, "Mama! Mama!" Mother said those were the sweetest words she ever heard. Dr. Mitzner then prayed for my eyesight, hearing, and other senses. He prayed for every part of my body. He said that altogether it took about forty-five minutes. When he finished praying for me, I got up and started running around the house, completely healed!

When my brother Charles was born at Big Sisters Hospital in Ventura and was placed in mother's arms for the first time, she looked heavenward and prayed,

"Lord, I promised to give You my life and dedicate myself to Your ministry. And God, I will fulfill to You my promise in this son that You have given me to do what I said I would do."

Mother wisely never told my brother of her promise to the Lord. When he was a teenager, he came home from church summer camp and told mother of his encounter with the Lord and the call he felt on his life for full-time service. It wasn't until my brother went to Bible college some years later that my mother told him of her vow to God. She wanted him to be certain in his own heart that this was God's leading.

I only wish my mother and father had lived to see the ministry that has touched people all over the world. I can't help but wonder, however, if my mother is looking down now and remembering the day she held her baby son, Charles (Chuck) Smith, in her arms and dedicated him to His service.

CHAPTER 33

A YOUNG MOTHER CONTENDS FOR TWO LIVES

W HAT FOLLOWS IS A first-person account from Kari, one of our young ladies, who grew up in the church from early childhood.

In July 1989, I was diagnosed with cervical cancer. At the same time, I also discovered that I was two months pregnant. My doctor…advised me to have an abortion so that I could immediately go in for surgery. He told me that going through the gestation period of a full-term pregnancy would most likely turn the cancer invasive, and it could take my life.

I decided that I wanted to go through with the pregnancy, and Pastor Risser said he would support my decision. During the next Sunday morning service, he called me to the front of the church and had several women of the church—as well as family members and some elders—anoint me with oil, lay hands on me, and pray for my healing.

In the Sunday night service, there was a guest speaker: Father Victor Alfonzo, a charismatic Catholic priest from India. As he was prophesying over individuals in the congregation, he began describing in detail a young woman who had "some female complications." He went on to say, "The Lord's peace is coming down upon the top of your head and enveloping your body, and the Lord is healing you."

I began looking all around the congregation wondering who he might be talking about. As I was searching the audience, all of a sudden I felt this peace come over the top of my head. Just as quickly, it dawned on me, "It's *me*. The problem he just described is what I'm going through." I felt the Lord working in my life, and I felt His healing power.

My doctor told me that I would need to have surgery approximately six weeks after giving birth. I gave birth to my son, Nick, and six weeks later I went back to the doctor's office, where he administered the same test that he had originally administered, which diagnosed the cancer.

This time, however, no cancer cells were present. He called me into his office and admitted that he didn't understand what had happened. The cancer was nowhere to be found.

I was so excited and told him, "My church prayed for me, and the Lord healed me!"

"Well," he said, "that's nice, Kari. But I still trust the original diagnosis. I am still recommending that you have surgery." I was so disappointed. As much as I tried to convince him of my healing, he kept insisting that the doctor who had originally administered the test was very reputable, and he could not deny the original diagnosis.

Oh, me of little faith! I agreed to the surgery, which did not go so well. Two weeks later, I was back in the hospital for emergency follow-up surgery. Off and on I have had complications as a result of this surgery.

And it never needed to happen at all.

The results from the surgery proved once again that the Lord had indeed healed me. There was no trace of cancer *at all*.

I thank the Lord for my healing and for my wonderful son, Nick, who has been a dream come true. Nick is now sixteen and is such a blessing in my life. He is a spiritually sensitive young man, shows a deep love for the Lord, and senses God's call on his life to be a pastor. I can hardly wait to see how the Lord plans to use this life that Satan was so determined to destroy.

CHAPTER 34

OUR PREACHER DIES AT THE PULPIT

I T WAS FRIDAY NIGHT toward the end of a spiritual emphasis week at our church in Santa Fe Springs. There were up to 450 people in attendance.

The speaker that night was Rev. Milton Ellithorpe, an outstanding preacher—one of my favorites since dating back to when he preached in my dad's church.

On this particular Friday night, however, two of my sons were playing in what had been billed as their local high school's football game of the year. I knew my priorities; I was senior pastor and had to be present at the service. But I also wanted to expedite things, if I could, to be able to attend some of the game's final quarter.

As it turned out, football was out of the question on that fateful Friday night. Events, as they say, overtook us.

It wasn't Milton's fault. Fully appreciative of my desire to get to the game, the preacher had given me permission to slip out during the post-service prayers for people in need, letting my able pastoral staff fill in for me.

I glanced at my watch as Milton was building up to his final salvation invitation, noting we were ahead of schedule. As always, he was bold and forceful in his call. I can close my eyes right now and hear his voice.

> I want *everyone* in this church building to close your two eyes, and *don't you dare* look around! That goes for all the ushers and ministerial staff. Head usher in the back, that goes for you, too.

After the invitation for people to raise their hands in response to his appeal, he said, "As we sing 'Just as I Am,' I'm inviting those of you who raised your hands to come forward and kneel right here at the altar. There are folks here right now who are prepared to pray with you and lead you to the Lord."

Just before we sang, however, Pastor Ellithorpe did something completely uncharacteristic for him. He pulled a chair over to the side of the pulpit, looked right at me, and said, "Pastor, you come."

Why would he call me to come forward? That wasn't his style.

Nevertheless, sensing something of his urgency, I moved toward him. Standing on the floor level of the sanctuary, I was face to face with the preacher. He had seated himself in the chair by the pulpit, and when he motioned me to lean over he whispered, with all dignity and composure, "I'm having a heart attack!"

Just that quickly, he made a gargling noise in his throat, his head dropped to his chest, *and he died.*

I quickly felt for a pulse on his neck, but there was nothing. I had played enough sports to be good at picking up a pulse and knew very well he had none at all. As the paramedics would soon confirm, the preacher had died beside the pulpit.

I looked around for help, but Pastor Ellithorpe had set the rules firmly. There wasn't a single eye open in the whole sanctuary! About a dozen people were responding to the invitation to receive Christ as the hymn went on and on. I had thought that "Just as I Am" was a brief song, but that night I came to find it to be the longest song in the hymnal. This was trauma at its worst.

Here's how it shaped up:

- The visiting evangelist, one of my dearest friends, had died in the chair by the pulpit.
- People were responding to his final invitation, wanting to receive Christ.
- The invitation hymn seemed to have 17 verses and went on forever.
- I needed help in the worst way, but 450 people in the auditorium had their eyes tightly closed.
- I had to literally hold Pastor Ellithorpe upright in his chair, or he would have fallen several feet to the floor.

In that moment, the words of my preacher father came back to me. "Stay calm under pressure, and you will make better decisions."

Finally, the song was over, and I caught the eyes of my alert staff members Dave and John. They told me later they had cheated by peeking out of one eye. I asked John to take my wife and Mrs. Ellithorpe out of the sanctuary. In the meantime, I directed Dave to gather some men at the front of the sanctuary and carry Pastor Ellithorpe, chair and all, back into the prayer room. Those men proved to be steller. We had just developed an extensive emergency plan that would serve us in times like this. The only glitch was that it was designed for people in the congregation at Sunday services but not for the preacher who died at the pulpit on Friday night. That proved to be the delay in calling the paramedics.

When they arrived, they declaring him to be a straight-liner, meaning he had no heartbeat; he was dead. They pulled out the paddles and shocked him with their defibrillator, once and twice. There was no response. Finally, they gave him the maximum application, and this brought about the weakest of pulse. They conveyed him to a nearby hospital.

Meanwhile, the congregation became aware of the emergency, and I had to report to them of Milton Ellithorpe's condition. Immediately, most of the church surged to the front for prayer. What followed was an urgent and effectual prayer meeting, which, in my opinion, had a real bearing on the ultimate outcome.

After an hour I dismissed the congregation, telling them to pray if and when they awakened in the night and to call the church tomorrow morning for an update. Several of the men stayed and prayed through the night.

I left for the hospital and arrived just in time to hear a report from the medical team. The doctors said that there were two things working against the patient's survival. First, his heart attack had caused irreparable damage. Second, there was every indication that the patient had gone so long without oxygen that even if he survived, the brain damage he suffered would disable him from almost all his physical functions.

I still remember the doctor's chilling words: "It is my experience that a person who has suffered this kind of trauma could quite possibly not make it through the night."

I felt inclined to rebuke an overzealous man, a pushy man who was new to our congregation, when he suddenly interrupted the doctor, showing more anger than wisdom. With a fighting attitude He said, "He's *not* going to die, because we believe in miracles, and we expect God to heal him." He went to express criticism because this doctor was "taking away our faith."

Undeterred, the doctor replied that if Pastor Ellithorpe survived in a vegetative state, it would be a condition worse than death. "And God knows that, too!" he added.

I determined to keep those kinds of people out of the hospital in times of crisis, since they think they are showing their faith by picking a fight with medical doctors who give us a diagnosis that we don't want to hear. It is important for us to realize representatives from the medical profession are working as hard for our loved ones as we are praying for them. In a sense we should all be on the same team working toward the best outcome.

To everyone's relief, a couple of our young and strong men took him to the car and sent him home. The few of us who were left prayed for Pastor Ellithorpe's healing but added, "Lord, You know what is best. Please override us if we are missing what is best for our friend."

When I finally went home around 2:30 a.m., I was already grieving the loss of a friend, whether by death or disability.

I arrived at the hospital on Saturday morning prepared for the worst and, frankly, expecting the worst. He would probably be in a coma, I reasoned, kept alive by a mass of tubes sprouting from life-support machines.

Instead, I encountered him sitting up in bed, looking as bright and rested as though he had just awakened from a nap.

"Paul Risser!" he boomed. "What are you doing here?"

I stopped just inside the doorway, frozen for a moment in disbelief.

"I can't believe that you came all this way to see me," he said, smiling broadly. "I will never forget this!"

Milton had been told he'd had suffered a traumatic heart attack the night before, but he was confused as to where he was. He thought he was back East and that I had rushed back to see him. "You are the most kind man," he told me. I took full credit.

"Milton," I stammered, "how are you feeling?"

"I feel perfectly fine," he said. Anyone looking at him in that moment would have to conclude that he spoke the truth.

I returned to the hospital later that afternoon to check his status. This time his mind was clear as a bell, and he was aware of everything that had happened to him. More than anything, he was happy that twelve people came to the Lord after he died momentarily.

In his meeting with the cardiac specialist at noon, the doctor had told him they could find no evidence of any heart damage. In fact, Ellithorpe beamed, "They may release me today!" When I couldn't find a reply, he added, "I could be available to preach again tomorrow at the church."

This time I laughed.

"I don't care what your doctor says," I told him, "you can't preach tomorrow. You may have recovered from what happened last night, but *I have not!*" After a moment's pause, I added, "Milton, do you realize what happened last night? Do you understand that you died on the platform, and I had to hold your body in the chair while people were coming to receive Christ and the church was singing, 'Just as I Am'? Do you have any recollection of that?"

"No," he said, "I don't. And I didn't have any out-of-body experience, either."

He came back one Sunday later and preached several times without one glitch.

Some time later, Pastor Ellithorpe was invited to speak to a group of cardiologists from the University of Southern California Medical Center. Sixty cardiologists came together to observe and interview Milton Ellithorpe. How had he survived? How was it that there had been no heart damage, no brain damage, no visible physical manifestations at all from his extended period of time without oxygen? They respectfully listened as he made the point that it could only be accounted as a miracle from God. The evidence was apparent, but as is always the case, some believed in what he said and others didn't.

Ellithorpe went on to live for exactly one year. He was walking in the park in Moline, Illinois, where he was conducting services at Moline Gospel Temple, when he suffered a heart attack. This one was fatal.

I will not be so arrogant to pretend to have an explanation for the way God works. I can only say that this miracle impacted hundreds of people who had a close of view of the glory of God.

CHAPTER 35

DIVINE HORSE SENSE

THE RISSER FAMILY AND Nina share grandchildren together, and I always talk to her about her memories of being a little girl in the middle of World War II. Her country, the Ukraine, was surrounded and covered by some of the most ruthless regimes in the history of the world. Ten million Ukrainian people were killed by the Russians alone. The Iwanczuk family would have been among those if it had not been for the grace of God, protection, provisions, direction, and wisdom. Here I will only focus on their miraculous escape, when there was danger on every side.

೮೩

Nina Iwanczuk was six years old and living with her family in the Ukraine when World War II broke out.

Early in his life, Nina's father had journeyed to America to make some money, with the plan to return to the Ukraine and start a business. As it turned out, however, the greatest thing that happened to him in America wasn't financial. While he was in the U.S. he came under the influence of Christian people and found Jesus Christ as his Savior. He happily returned home with capital to launch his new business and, more importantly, with a relationship with God.

The first thing he did was lead his immediate and extended family to Christ, teaching them how a powerful, loving God was engaged in the details of their everyday lives and cared about their future.

With war raging on all sides, they found themselves in the eye of the tornado. Although danger was on every hand—and many times they wondered how they would survive—the family experienced daily protection, direction, provision, courage, and strength. Through it all, they prayed that God would use their family as an instrument of blessing to people who were more endangered than they were because of their ethnicity or nationalities. On numerous occasions, they hid Jewish or German neighbors in their homes to protect them from certain death at the hands of vengeful Russian soldiers.

Then came the day when the Russians authorities approached Nina's father, insisting that he become a spy. Being a man of conviction, he adamantly refused. As a result, the Russian marked him as an enemy and a traitor. Later that day he got word from a trusted friend in the know that the next day their entire family was to be taken to Siberia—and certain death. Siberia meant to them what the ovens meant to the Jews.

"Many of our friends and neighbors were banished to Siberia," Nina recalls, "and we never knew of anyone who returned."

After urgent prayer the family concluded that they would have to flee for their lives. But how? And where? With no good options, it seemed best to them to attempt an escape through Poland—even though that nation was also hostile to Ukrainians. Nina's father and uncle, however, had gone to school in Poland and were articulate in Polish, which would give them a decided advantage.

From there, they felt the Lord was putting it in their hearts to make their way through Germany, concluding that such a route would be safer for them, since the Americans and Allied forces were close to defeating Germany. Also, word was out that the Americans were compassionate toward "DPs" (displaced persons), people who had been forced to leave their countries.

There was no time to ponder the merits of the decision, because it was now a matter of life or death. One false move, one wrong turn, would be the end for them.

Just before setting out the next morning, they prayed for the Lord's direction, and that His blood would cover them from danger and take them safely to Germany.

As quickly and secretly as they knew how, they had conspired to travel with two other Ukrainian families. One man was particularly important because he knew the route to their destination. They arranged to meet at a fork in the road at a certain time early in the morning. The Iwanczuks arrived at the set time, but where were the other families? They never came, and no one ever heard what had happened to them.

So there they were, at a fork in the road with no maps or signposts! Which route would take them to safety? No one in the family had any idea. Waiting, however, wasn't an option. The authorities might already be looking for them. But if they took the wrong road, they might never reach their destination. Nina remembers the most abbreviated—and meaningful—prayer meeting her family had ever experienced. Her father prayed the prayer of David in Psalm 25:4: "Show me Your ways, O LORD; teach me Your paths."

Every member of the family understood the consequences of going down a wrong road. Nina and the surviving members of the family today still recall vividly that just before their father finished praying, the two very gentle horses started moving forward in synch, completely of their own initiative, on the road to the left.

Nina's dad was spiritually sensitive enough to understand that God had used the most unconventional way to get them on the right road—by putting the direction into the instincts of the horses!

Traveling through Poland was terrifying, but no one stopped or questioned them along the way. They arrived at the Warsaw train depot just in time to catch the very last train out of Poland toward Munich, Germany. On the train they conversed with other Ukrainians about their journey out of their homeland, telling of the two families who never arrived and the dilemma over which direction to take at the crossroads. Then they related the experience with the horses taking the left fork without anyone's hands on the reins.

One of their traveling companions listened in wonder and shook his head. If they had taken the right fork, he told them, they would have been doomed. A big bridge on that road had been destroyed, and the route was impassable.

Reaching Munich, the Iwanczuks were able to stay in a compound provided by an American Baptist organization. The experience of their journey from Ukraine to Munich convinced every member of that family an almighty God gave such careful attention to every aspect of their lives.

As the prophet Isaiah told the Israelites of old, "Whether you turn to the right or to the left, your ears will hear a voice behind you, saying, 'This is the way; walk in it'" (Isa. 30:21).

Only in this case, the Lord spoke that word into the ears of two horses!

> Help us choose the right way, Jesus,
> Avoiding dangers that await.
> For when we follow where you lead us,
> Our paths are always straight.
>
> —Ellen Hagemeyer

CHAPTER 36

JESUS ALREADY TOLD ME

IN MY FIRST PASTORATE we had a grand older couple who we affectionately referred to as Brother and Sister Moore. They were fun people and enjoyed life to the fullest. Their friendliness, sense of humor, and love of life had made their humble little house a gathering place, where everybody in the neighborhood liked to stop by to be touched by their joy.

I have to admit that if ever I became discouraged I would debate as to whether I should spend an hour in prayer or go spend an hour with the Moores. Every time I did go see them, I came away feeling renewed. By far however, the biggest story of Brother and Sister Moore's lives was their love for the Lord. They were forthright and genuine followers of Christ.

Beyond their love for Jesus, the thing that impressed me most about them was their obvious love of each other. Even though they had been married well over fifty years, they still teased each other like a couple of teenagers. They loved being together and seemed to be inseparable.

In his youth, Brother Moore had been an outstanding second baseman and had always kept his great love for sports. Every Monday night during volleyball season, he had made it his habit to come to the high school to watch our team play. After the game, he got into his car to head for home. That night, as he came to a stop at a certain intersection, he suddenly suffered a fatal stroke. He laid his head on the steering wheel and was gone in an instant.

A team of paramedics rushed him to the hospital, but he was pronounced dead on arrival. A police officer came to the high school, where I was still visiting with some people, to give me the news that Mr. Moore had suffered a stroke and was in the hospital. I ran to my car and rushed to see him but was grieved to learn he had already died.

I can't begin to explain how sad I felt. Brother and Sister Moore meant the world to me in those first years of my pastorate. They were my best encouragement. I was stunned and grieved.

The doctor, whom I knew well from the Rotary Club, quietly told me, "Paul, you should be the one to go and break the news to Mrs. Moore."

I immediately thought, "If I feel this overwhelmed, how will this hit Sister Moore? Maybe she'll have a stroke, too!"

I would rather have done almost anything than break this news to Sister Moore about the love of her life. How could I do this? What if she were utterly overcome? What would I do? I had grown up as a pastor's kid and had accompanied my dad in almost every possible situation, but when I tried to think about how he would have handled it, my mind went blank.

Suddenly a thought came to me, bringing with it a quick flood of hope. "I'll call their daughter!" I told myself. I knew her to be a strong, stable Christian woman who could bolster and sustain her mother during this time. As I went to the phone, I thanked the Lord over and over for giving me this brilliant idea. Hallelujah, my problem was solved.

Not quite.

In fact, the daughter wasn't home. Now what was I to do?

I stalled for time by going into the room where Brother Moore's body laid covered with a blanket. I had the secret wish he could rise from the dead so I wouldn't have to tell the bad news to Sister Moore.

I stalled longer, trying to think of another answer—some way out of the situation. I called the daughter once more, but the phone just rang and rang. No one was going to answer. She wasn't home, and I knew I would have to face Mrs. Moore.

I ran into the doctor in the hall of the hospital as he was still making his rounds. He looked up at me with surprise, and I could read his expression like a book. "What are you doing here? You mean you still haven't gone to tell Mrs. Moore?"

The guilt I felt from that encounter gave me the impetus to leave the hospital and go to their home. Driving exceptionally slowly, I tried to use the time to think of the words I would speak to Sister Moore when she opened the door. What could I say that would keep her from completely falling apart?

When I stopped in front of her house, my heart was pounding like a hammer in my chest. I lost my breath to the point that I almost couldn't speak. But what difference would that make? I had no idea what to say to her anyway. As I looked up at the Moores' house, I noticed that Sister Moore was standing at the door, holding it open for me. She asked, "Something happened to Daddy, didn't it?"

All I could do was nod my head yes, and I began to cry. With sympathy for me, she continued, "Don't worry about it, honey. It will be OK, because Jesus has already come and told me about it." And then she reached her arms around me and prayed that I would be all right.

As a young pastor I had so much to learn, and I daily asked the Holy Spirit to show me the glory of Christ in the everyday life of my church. In this case, He showed me the fulfillment of Paul's words in Philippians 4:6–7:

> Do not be anxious about anything, but in everything, by prayer and petition, with thanksgiving, present your requests to God. And the peace of God, which transcends all understanding, will guard your hearts and your minds in Christ Jesus.

This literally means that God will calm you at a time you should naturally be upset and devastated. I learned that truth on Sister Moore's front porch, on a day when in my sorrow and fear I couldn't find words of comfort but received comfort instead.

CHAPTER 37

FINDING LESLIE KEEGLE

B ACK IN THE EARLY 1980s, when Marilee and I, along with two close friends, Jeanne and Betty, were preparing an itinerary to visit churches in Asia, I dialed Leslie and Belen Keegle's phone number in Sri Lanka to see if we could spend a little time with him. Leslie was the national director of our church in that nation, at that time numbering something around eight hundred. (Today that number has grown to over fourteen hundred.)

After numerous calls, however, we could never get through to Leslie. His fellow leaders in the area assured us that as far as they knew he was home and could be located. Even so, I cringed a bit when we added Sri Lanka to our itinerary. What if he really wasn't in the country? What if we couldn't track him down? What a waste of time and money that would be!

Our group of four finally arrived in Colombo and checked in to our hotel. It was a rough night for me. I couldn't seem to shake my anxiety over tracking down Leslie. We had a vague-sounding address but no real directions at all. Tossing and turning through the night, I prayed that God would direct our steps. I had a strong sense that we were in Sri Lanka for a reason, but at that point, I wasn't sure what it might be.

Out in front of the hotel that morning, there were at least twenty taxi drivers, all anxious to get hires. I kept a twenty dollar bill in my hand as an extra incentive for these highly competitive cabbies to help me find Leslie. But not one of those drivers recognized the address we'd been given. They wanted the fare but could only shrug their shoulders. None of them had ever heard of such a location.

How could this be? My heart sank with disappointment as I walked back to the hotel entrance. It was exactly what I had been afraid of! And now what? How could the four of us make the most of a day in Colombo? Apparently I had wasted everyone's time with a wild goose chase.

Just as I was about to walk back into the lobby, however, one of the taxi drivers came running up to me. Another driver had just come from the airport; maybe he would be able to recognize the mysterious address. At that point, I wasn't overly confident of success. If twenty drivers couldn't make heads or tails of it, why should number twenty-one?

This driver, however, knew the address instantly.

"Of course I know," he said. "That is the neighborhood where I grew up, and I know exactly where he lives. This man is a religious man, very quiet, and has a friendly Filipino wife."

Apparently, the "address" I'd been given wasn't a proper address at all. It described a landmark—a particular, distinctive *tree*—and not a street or number. And this one taxi driver, out of a city of multiple millions of people, knew where Leslie lived. I felt ashamed over my lack of faith in the Lord's direction.

Leslie greeted us with wide-eyed surprise and joy. He was just beginning a week of fasting and prayer, and when he saw us, he felt sure that the Lord had already answered his prayers.

It didn't take us long to learn that Leslie was in a severe predicament. In his tenure as national director in Sri Lanka,

Leslie had seen the number of churches grow from ten little fledgling congregations to over eight hundred churches. What they desperately needed now was a prominent headquarters centrally located in the city, with accompanying facilities for a pastors' training center.

And Leslie had found—or, rather, thought he had found—exactly what was needed. In one of the listings of current property offerings, he had come across a reasonably priced piece of land in a prime location, at a central hub in Colombo. Digging further, Leslie's excitement grew. The property was accessible by public transportation from anywhere in the city. In fact, that particular tract of land was part of a master plan for a reconfiguration of central Colombo.

Talk about ideal! The lot was substantial enough for a sizable sanctuary, as well as an adjoining training center for Sri Lankan pastors. What an opportunity to advance the gospel in Sri Lanka! How could he miss such an opportunity? Several other interested parties had already inquired about the land, and Leslie knew he had to act fast or the window would close.

Yes, he realized that officially he would need denominational board approval to make such a commitment. But in those days there were no e-mails, no cell phones, and even telephone connections could be iffy. In fact, he'd tried to reach Los Angeles all day after finding the property and couldn't get a call through.

Should he sign the papers, trusting that the denomination would share his excitement over the property and come through with the needed funds? He felt almost sure they would. But should he take the risk and put down money without board approval?

Swallowing hard, Leslie went ahead and made a deposit on the land. A few days later, however, he had grave second thoughts about his decision, as the reality of Sri Lanka's strict property laws began to sink in. If he didn't come up with the full amount of money to purchase the land by a certain date, he would face large fines—and possibly imprisonment.

Leslie had climbed out on the end of a long limb and felt more than a little queasy about it. Feeling that he might be in real trouble, he had started his week of fasting and praying. And before the first day was out, we showed up on his doorstep!

What's more, later he told me that as we greeted each other I had said to him, "We want to see your property!" But I never remembered saying anything like that; I didn't even know about any property at that point.

I did know something, however, that Leslie didn't know. As a member of our denomination's board, I was aware of a new policy: the U.S. church would no longer provide the finances for the 120–plus national churches we had around the world at that time. Part of the reason for the trip was to break that bit of unhappy news to our national directors.

But surely common sense would compel us to make an invest-ment in a fast-growing national church that would someday number in the thousands of congregations. And besides that, we had to keep our national director out of jail! I quickly assured Leslie and Belin that our Florence Avenue church would help raise money. Also we would petition the board to waive the moratorium on finances in this case. After all, Leslie hadn't even heard of the policy when he took his leap of faith.

Within a week after returning from Sri Lanka, I presented this opportunity to the board. With the encouragement of venerable leaders such a Dr. Leland Edwards and Dr. Courtney, it was passed unanimously.

In the years since acquiring that property, the training center has produced hundreds of pastors, and the church has burgeoned into a thriving congregation of mostly business-people and professional people who have assumed much of the financial and spiritual responsibility of our exponential growth in the country and region.

Leslie's faith was rewarded, and I was grateful that the Lord had made sense of what I had been convinced was a bumbling mistake and a waste of time.

CHAPTER 38

DIVINE SHORTCUTS

W HEN SOME OF US were in denominational leadership, we decided that we wanted to make the first board motion toward the establishment of a pastor and church personnel retirement plan.

Because of my naiveté to all the government regulations, I assumed that one would wave a magic wand and it would come into being. I got a dose of reality when all the experts gathered around the table with us and explained that at best this plan could be up and running in four years.

Because we had such a desire to get it in effect immediately, and impatient as I am, I was disheartened. Nonetheless, I went home in the evening and called some of our most diligent men of prayer at Florence Avenue, several of them very young, to pray that God would help speed the process.

We prayed John 6:21. It is the miracle of Jesus calming the storm. It says, "Then they were eager to let him in the boat, and immediately they arrived at their destination!" (NLT). Many cessationist scholars, those who believe that no more miracles happened after the death of the apostles, argue they didn't immediately arrive at land but that with Jesus in the boat it just seemed like a short distance. But theologians like John Phillips say we should not quibble on the statement, since sometimes the Lord transcends time and distances; we should accept that passage at its face value. We who believe Hebrews 13:8, which tells us Jesus Christ is the same yesterday, today, and forever, believe that He has the ability to circumvent processes today.

Accordingly, some of us dared to pray that God would abbreviate or hasten the normal process of setting up the retirement plan.

In response to our prayers, God miraculously sent Charlie Cammack to us. He was an acquaintance of one of everybody's favorites, the late Dick Schmidt. Charlie was widely known in Washington, D.C., for being the foremost authority on religious retirement plans. It seemed he had a mental grasp of the retirement plan offered by every denomination in America. He agreed to meet with us, and afterward he teamed with his lawyer and returned to Washington to begin working on our behalf. They agreed to expedite everything we needed. In addition, Charlie agreed to come to every one of our meetings at no expense. (He was accustomed to making $150 an hour.)

God gave us such favor with Charlie. When the plan went into effect, it had taken us exactly one year, thanks to Charlie and to our great committee and, of course, to the Lord.

Recently, I called Charlie to get the details of what I thought was a miraculous story directly from him. "It always takes at least four years, sometimes five," Charlie verified. "But with Foursquare it only took one." We set a speed record. He told me, "The Lord was with you." Charlie showed his favor by saying, "I was as happy for you as I would have been for my own Episcopalian denomination."

There is no limit to the creative ways that God works.

CHAPTER 39

THE EFFECTUAL PRAYER OF MR. SPAN

In his heart a man plans his course, but the LORD
determines his steps

—PROVERBS 16:9

ONE AFTERNOON I WAS visiting with missionary Frank
Ziegler at the missionary compound in Willowvale,
Transkei, South Africa. We were sitting in his attic, going
through pictures that told the story of four and one-half decades
of his ministry in the Transkei.

If, as a tourist, I was struck with the remoteness of this mission
station, I was thoroughly overcome as the pictures revealed the
primitive condition of that part of the world when they arrived
in 1929. The skillful Ziegler had laid out the little town himself,
providing both a water and electrical system.

With his wife and family, Brother Ziegler had given himself
with agape love for the Xhosa tribal people. I was aware of the
fact that our denomination had not brought the Ziegler family
home for their scheduled five-year furloughs through their first
twenty years there.

When you think about it, however, it made sense. The voyage
by ship to America would have taken so long that they would

have had to turn around and head back to Africa almost as soon as they arrived.

Leafing through those remarkable pictures in his attic, I asked him, "Frank, this is like the 'uttermost part of the earth.' *How in the world did you find these people?*"

Ziegler's sharp German-featured face lit up with joy at my question, and I could see he had a story to tell, a story of the amazing providence of God.

Frank Ziegler had every reason to believe in miracles, right from the start.

MR. SPAN

It all started with a Dutch blacksmith and trader named Mr. Span, who made cooking pans and ironworks and provided goods and services to the Xhosa tribe in the Transkei province of South Africa. He had a real love for these people, who were dear to him, and being the Christian man he was, saw them facing the serious rigors of life without the knowledge or help of God.

Mr. Span did a great deal of praying for and with the Xhosa, but his consistent request was that God would send a missionary to teach them the ways of the Lord. He prayed every morning, over and over, until he finally heard in his heart what he perceived to be an answer from the Lord: *You don't have to pray anymore, because I will send you a missionary.*

James 5:16 says, "The earnest prayer of a righteous person has great power and produces wonderful results" (NLT).

Relieved and happy because of this word, he walked out of his home and looked off into the distance. Up in the sky, he saw a billowy cloud beginning to form the likeness of a man's face.

It was very clear, and the facial features were etched into Mr. Span's mind. He instantly understood that this man was going to be the answer to his prayer.

THE OREGON CONNECTION

The answer to Mr. Span's prayer began in the little town of Dayton, Oregon. A young lady, Dorothy Lewis, had recently graduated from the university and had started her career as a schoolteacher. At her church, she was attending a series of services when one night she was impressed by the Lord that He was going to change the direction of her life to that of a missionary. Coinciding with that message, she had a vision of black people laboring in a rolling green field. She took that as a calling to become a missionary in Africa.

The very next morning, she came across the very first edition of our denominational magazine and noticed an advertisement on the back cover. It was an ad promoting the newly opened LIFE Bible College in Los Angeles, where they prepared people to become pastors, evangelists, and missionaries. She interpreted that as the direction of the Lord to prepare for missionary work, so she proceeded to enroll at the college and moved to Los Angeles. Her parents, who had just provided the finances for her university education, were none too happy about this new direction (and additional schooling) but finally relented.

A YOUNG MAN FROM PASADENA

Frank was the son of an immigrant family who came to the United States from South Africa in the mid-1920s. Their first stop was in Missouri, and then they continued on to their final destination: Los Angeles. The family lived in Pasadena, and one Sunday night, Frank and his brother came to Los Angeles to go to the movies. They made one of those divine mistakes by thinking Angelus Temple was a theater, with the marquee that marked the entrance.

Even though they thought it was strange that no one was taking tickets, the Ziegler brothers walked into the auditorium and took their seats. When the music and worship began, they realized that they'd stumbled into a church instead of a theater. Seeing their mistake, they might have easily got up and left. But they couldn't help but be intrigued by the excitement these people had for their Christianity. If this was church, they'd never seen anything like it.

They decided to stay.

At the end of the service, Frank went forward at the invitation of the preacher and gave his life to Jesus Christ. He followed through on that commitment, becoming more and more involved at Angelus Temple, and it wasn't long until he had enrolled at LIFE Bible College.

FRANK MEETS DOROTHY

As you may have surmised, Frank met Dorothy at college and liked what he saw. When he discovered she was called to be a missionary to Africa, however, he almost lost interest in her. He had no desire, in the least, to return to the country from which he had so joyfully emigrated.

As he spent time with Dorothy, however, Frank began to feel a nudging in his own heart to return to South Africa as a missionary.

Frank and Dorothy eventually graduated together and were

married, but they delayed leaving for the mission field. Frank had been hired by the Ford Motor Company, which had a large facility in Los Angeles at the time. Because he was so competent in the field of engineering and mechanics, he moved right up the ladder. The couple began making more money than they had ever imagined and purchased an exceptionally nice house.

FRANK TURNS COLD, BUT GOD DEALT WITH HIM

In the process of reaping the benefits of an American success story, however, Frank's success began to dull his love for the Lord and particularly his calling to Africa. Moving to Africa seemed less and less like a reality with each passing day.

A sad chapter of their lives was that Frank lost his job in an economic downturn, which resulted in losing their house. This was mind-boggling to Frank, to the point he asked God why He seemed to be letting him lose so much. It came to his mind that the Lord was saying, *You will lose more if you don't get back on track to do My will for your life.*

CONNECTING WITH MR. SPAN

Frank humbled himself, and several years after God assured Mr. Span that his prayers had been heard, the Zieglers left on their missionary journey to South Africa. At that time, their family included three daughters, and Dorothy was expecting another child.

It is significant that Mrs. Ziegler gave birth to her first baby boy, Lewis, just two hours after arriving at port in Capetown. Because he was born on South African soil, Lewis Ziegler received dual citizenship. This proved extremely helpful as the years went on; in his twenties, Lewis became the full-fledged leader of the missions work in the Transkei, continuing the work of his father. Visas and in-and-out privileges were never a problem to Lewis.

The family stayed a few months with grandparents until the baby was old enough and strong enough to travel. During that time, the Zieglers were at a loss as to where, in this huge country, to start their missionary endeavors. This has been a matter of concern and prayer for them ever since they left for South Africa.

Nearly a thousand miles away from where Mr. Span had prayed—and received—the promise of a missionary, the Zieglers, however, knew nothing of this. It was up to God to somehow make the travel connections. And that is exactly what He did through a sequence of miracles.

The Lord had put it into Frank Ziegler's heart to take his wife and four children, get on a train, and head east. The divine directions were no more specific than that: head east. And they did. They went east and east and east, on one train line after another. Finally, after what seemed to be an endless trip, they entered the Transkei province. Ziegler heard the voice of the Lord in his heart that they were to get off at the first stop in the morning, a town called Butterworth.

Within a few miles of this destination, Dorothy, worn out as she was from this demanding trip, looked out the window and saw green rolling hills with black people everywhere. It was the exact vision she had seen several years ago in her home church in Dayton, Oregon.

As the Zieglers began gathering their things on the train,

preparing to disembark at what they believed to be their destination, Mr. Span was working in his shop, feeling a strange restlessness. Though he didn't know why, he felt a strong urge to leave his shop and go meet the train at the station.

Obedient to that stirring, Mr. Span stood and watched the passengers stepping out of the train car. Suddenly, he saw Frank Ziegler—the very image of the man he had seen in the clouds years before. Mr. Span stepped up and excitedly received the family, taking them to his home and letting them know of his prayers for a missionary and the image he saw of Ziegler in the cloud.

They were all feeling good about the fulfillment of God's plan. Mr. Span and the Zieglers began a working relationship that continued for over thirty years. They established churches all over the Transkei and became a spiritual force in that remote region that seemed to be forgotten to the rest of the world—but was known to God!

When Mr. Span told the Zieglers the story of his prayer and vision, Dorothy thought back and realized that this was the very time when she had received her call to missionary service back in Oregon. This was a grand affirmation to the Zieglers that they were truly in the center of God's will.

God had a plan, and He worked it from one side of the world to another!

CHAPTER 40

TRIUMPHANT AGAINST ALL ODDS

I N THE LATE 1940S Harold and Mary Williams and their children spent four years as missionaries in Bolivia. For their last year of their five-year term they moved to Brazil as our first missionaries to that country. Our hope was that they would be able to determine whether or not there would be any way of breaking what seemed like impossible barriers in order to get a foothold to establish a movement in that great country.

During that year they realized they were up against a formidable wall.

At the time, Brazil was the most Catholic country in the world, with 98 percent of the population being Catholic. The Catholic Church was not just a denomination but the state church, which made them not just a church but also a political power.

This type of relationship between the religious authorities and the government is the case in many countries of the world today. That is why the most driving purpose of the founding fathers fleeing from Europe to America was freedom of religion. They set up the Constitution so that every person could worship according to the dictates of his or her heart and so that one denomination would not gain arbitrary political power.

But, I must add, that freedom of religion was not instituted in America to forbid the church from influencing our government but rather to keep the government from exercising power over the church.

In Brazil, the Williamses were finding themselves doing a lot of sowing and little reaping. After one year they had given it their best, but the results were sparse. It seemed to them that their potential field of work was only two percent of the population—and that small number had a chip on their shoulders toward religion.

When the Williamses came home on furlough, our denomination board was considering sending them to another country rather than returning them to Brazil, since their work didn't show much promise because of the religious adversity. The board thought sending the Williams family back to Brazil might be investing personnel and money in a field that would be nonproductive.

Nonetheless, Harold returned to the U.S. for their furlough with the full intention to equip himself to return to Brazil. He seemed to have an insight that there was the possibility for our missions endeavor to become a mighty spiritual force. The opposition he and his family had encountered did not swerve their zeal for being participants in a spiritual awakening. Harold saw that his mission in Brazil was to get a foothold that would be so founded in the Scriptures that it would stand strong for generations to come. Besides, they loved Brazil and couldn't think of abandoning the work there.

While on furlough, Harold attended Billy Graham and Oral Roberts crusades when those evangelists were both young men and in the prime of their ministry. He was getting great ideas that would be transferable to Brazil. One such concept dawned like a light in his mind one night at a Billy Graham Crusade that was being conducted in a tent. Harold thought, "Brazilians love circuses. I think they would be drawn to a circus tent for a revival."

I had a conversation in the 1980s with Dr. Howard Courtney, who was the vice president of the denomination at the time of Williams' request. He was a very practical man and told me years later, "I almost cringe when I think how close we came to denying Harold Williams the return to Brazil and the purchase of the tent. One of the best things we ever did was to align with Harold's vision. Can you imagine the loss we would have suffered, had we not accommodated the things he had seen in his heart? In the one year they had been there, their work resulted in a small church, but now they wanted a tent that would comfortably seat twelve hundred people. Potentially they could pack three thousand Brazilians in with standing room. They had to have a miracle of God, or this would be a colossal failure."

Dr. Courtney added that the board surmised that purchasing the tent could be a waste of limited resources since the denomination could have gone into three other receptive countries for what it would cost to return the Williamses to Brazil. The question was, Could this missionary endeavor overcome the gigantic barriers that will be placed on them?

GOD SEES FROM A DIFFERENT VANTAGE POINT

One thing I have noticed as I observe the way God works miracles is that often the magnitude of a miracle is not seen for years to come. The full effect is often invisible until you look in retrospect, because when they happen they often seem inconspicuous.

A biblical example is the story of Joseph. Between Genesis 37 and 40, we see him being sold as a slave to the Egyptians, then being the victim of the wrath of Potiphar's spurned wife, and then getting sent to prison. Little do we know until we get to the end of the story that every one of the aforementioned calamities became what we might call inverted miracles. Each of these apparent setbacks were miracles in the strangest ways. God used these apparent reverses as miracles to get Joseph to the fulfillment of the dreams he had as a boy, dreams that revealed God's ultimate plan. These tragedies were God's way of getting Joseph to his lofty position, from which he could spare the lives of his family.

We can't help but be emotional when we hear Joseph's words when he reveals his identity to his brothers: "You meant evil against me, but God meant it for good" (Gen. 50:20, NAS). We see things from alpha to omega, but God sees from omega to alpha. All along our life's journey He drops big, medium, and mustard seed sized miracles to help us realize His grand design as the Holy Spirit weaves His way through the course of our lives.

Mary Williams remembers that the Lord was putting it in Harold's heart that there was something special on the horizon, but he could not have anticipated the degree to which it would ultimately develop. Little did he know how God was using him and his wife to lay the foundation for a work that in five decades would number ten thousand churches, adherents totaling several million, and three hundred training centers strategically throughout Brazil. Because of their work, pastors and leaders are being equipped to helm churches that are part of the vision of today's generations. Even into the twenty-first century the momentum in Brazil continues.

Mary, who is now a clear-minded lady of ninety-eight years old, still holds great love in her heart for Brazil and its people. I speak with her frequently, and she offers an account of the Brazil awakening as though it were yesterday. I am amused that each time we speak Mary invariably ends our conversations saying, in effect, "I love each time when we can talk about Brazil. My, how Harold and I loved Brazil, and we loved Brazilians. I would give anything to be able to relive our years in Brazil. It was like a dream."

℣

There is not room in this book to write the full story of that great revival, but I am going to include two events that will give you the sense of the dimension of that revival.

A Miracle the Size of a Mustard Seed

While on furlough before the start of the revival, Harold was on an itinerary in the Midwest, where he stayed in the parsonage of a church in the area. During the morning when he was packing, the pastor walked into the room and pitched a booklet on top of his clothes. Harold put it in the back flap of the suitcase, which he seldom used, and closed his suitcase. A little miracle was in the making, but Williams had no idea. It would be six months before he recognized it.

When the Williams family returned to Sao Paulo, they began unpacking. Among other things, Harold was opening boxes and suitcases. Finally, he unpacked that suitcase he used on his itinerary where the pastor pitched in the booklet. Though checking the back flap was out of character, before he closed the suitcase and put it in the attic he reached into the flap and discovered that booklet from the pastor in America.

He couldn't ever remember how it got there. This book had seemed so insignificant when it was given to him that Harold forgot which pastor gave it to him, forgot the subject of the book, and had forgotten it was in his suitcase until he accidentally found it.

After he was through unpacking he was drawn to browse through the book, with no great interest. It was on a subject that was foreign to him, the importance of fasting and prayer. Even if the book was not a classic or written by a famous person, Williams couldn't put it down. He felt a strange impulse to read it through.

It seemed the Lord spoke to his heart as he was reading, "This is for you. It will be the key to your ministry in Brazil. Take this seriously." He couldn't imagine what great difference it would make, but the Lord impressed upon him two things:

- *I have given you the vision to see a little of what is ahead.*
- *Now, I am giving you the method for your empowerment.*

Before he arose from his chair, he determined to fast the next three days, which was Friday through Sunday. Through all of his fastings, he would go to each meal with the family and participate in conversation with his three children, John, Paul, and Diane.

That Sunday night Harold was scheduled to be the guest speaker at a Presbyterian church made up mostly of Americans working and living in Sao Paulo. The pastor and Harold were close friends. Harold was to speak on revival in the United States and planned to focus on the Billy Graham and Oral Roberts crusades.

When he returned from that Presbyterian service, he excitedly told Mary that he had never felt the anointing of the Holy Spirit on his preaching as he did that night. They had a conversation as to what could have made the difference. Mary suggested that it might have been his fasting and prayer. Harold knew that was it. He told Mary that starting the next Monday he was going to fast for a week. She volunteered to join him.

At the end of that fast, they observed that the anointing on their ministry increased. A few weeks later they began and completed a fourteen-day fast. The affects were beyond imagination. He was not only empowered, but he was surprised by a God-given comprehension of the Brazilian culture, along with ideas that could be put into effect immediately to help advance the upcoming revival.

Harold told Mary that he was going to fast for twenty-one days and then followed that fast shortly after with a forty-day fast.

Mary tells how people frequently ask, "What effect did Harold's fasting have on the Brazilian revival?" Her answer stays the same: "I don't know what his fasting did for Brazil; that is for others to say. But I do know what it did for Harold:

- "He prayed like no person I have ever heard pray.

- ♦ "He preached with an anointing and was powerful.
- ♦ "He had an added grasp of the Scripture that gave believers a greater foundation that had a long-lasting impact.
- ♦ "He gained spiritual gifts that enabled to him to recognize people who needed prayer and bring deliverance to a high number of demon-possessed individuals, though this affliction was, at the time, of epidemic proportion. (The mixture of voodoo with those who were lax in the Christian church made people especially susceptible to demonic power.)
- ♦ "He also showed the capacity to make many common-sense decisions, the practice of which are used by the church even today."

The Long Shadow Cast by Revival

I present this last story as an example of the lasting effect of the crusade that started in the late 1940s.

Just recently we were talking with a bivocational pastor/international banker from Sao Paulo and his wife, Sueli, also a pastor. They came down to Long Beach for dinner with our mission director's wife. During their visit, I was telling them of my interest in what I called the Williams Revival and what I had already written about the Williams Crusade, as I call it, in their city of Sao Paulo. I told them of the details I had learned during my eighteen trips to Brazil and through the perhaps more than thirty-five visits I had with Mary Williams in person or on the phone. As I was unfolding what I came to know, I could see Sueli getting emotional.

She began to tell us her firsthand knowledge of her family's experience with the Williams Revival. Long before Sueli was born, her grandmother developed a terminal illness and was expected to live only a short time. In her desperation, she visited a voodoo witch doctor with no results. Then a friend invited her to the tent where, she was told, they prayed for the sick. The friend told her that many of her neighbors had been healed there.

Sueli's grandmother was reluctant but went despite the fierce objection of her religiously devout husband. In the course of the service, Harold Williams stopped the service and spoke to the audience, "There is a lady visiting tonight who has an illness near unto death. You have gone to a voodoo doctor in desperation, but you have come here tonight for healing. And you are being healed right at this moment." Her grandma knew that at that very moment she was miraculously, fully healed. She went on to live for many years, and ultimately her husband came to the Lord.

Now, three generations later, her granddaughter is a minister in the Brazilian church movement that was founded in the tent crusade in which her grandmother and grandfather came to Christ. The impact of that spiritual awakening has moved from one generation to another.

CHAPTER 41

STORIES IN THE LIFE OF LOIS VAN CLEAVE

D R. NATHANIEL VAN CLEAVE was a venerable Bible scholar, professor, and a gentleman beloved by everyone who knew him. As a young man he heard the still, small voice speak to him about one day investing his life on the mission field.

It was a call, but not so strong that it became foremost in his mind. At least not yet.

As he began his pastoral ministry, he married Lois, the beautiful young lady of his dreams, who had grown up in a ministerial home led by a preaching grandfather. Through most of her years, her family had lived on the edge of poverty.

Though people would marvel at the profound preaching and teaching of Dr. Van Cleave, he never quite forgot the gentle tug on his heart toward missions he had experienced as a young man. In fact, it had been growing stronger through the years. The tug was becoming a *pull*.

But what would Lois say about it? He was almost sure she wouldn't like the idea. And how would he ever bring it up? He pushed the whole matter into the background (again), plunging into his role as a busy preacher and pastor.

Finally, after the Holy Spirit wouldn't seem to leave him

alone, he worked up the boldness to broach the subject with her, asking her if she had ever thought about the mission field.

Lois had an exceptional, outgoing personality and was never without an opinion. Those of us who knew her found her sense of humor a delight, and sometimes she seemed the funniest when she wasn't even trying.

In answer to her husband's tentative question, she said, in effect, "Well, you can forget *that* idea. I have lived off the bottom of the 'missionary barrel' all of my life, and I'm not going to put myself into that sort of predicament again."

Van Cleave knew he had touched a sensitive nerve, so he determined never to bring up the subject again—except to the Lord in prayer. He told God, "Well, Lord, I've heard Your call, and I am willing to go. But it will be up to You to put a willingness in Lois's heart, so I'll just leave it with You."

True to his decision, he never again raised the subject with her. A few months later, however, they attended a missionary conference where Dr. Van Cleave was a speaker. In his message, he said nothing at all about the inner call he had received earlier in life, even though the desire continued to burn strong and clear in his heart.

The evening they returned home from the conference, Lois came into the living room and sat on the arm of the recliner where her husband was sitting.

"God spoke to me at the conference," she told him.

"Oh? He did?"

"Yes, and He has called me to missions. So anytime you feel like we should go, let me know, because I'm ready."

After just a few weeks, Dr. Van Cleave got a phone call from the president of our denomination telling him of a need for a missionary in Puerto Rico and asked him if he and his wife would go. Lois had picked up the extension at some point during that conversation and had been listening in.

A deliberate, contemplative man, Dr. Van Cleave was never one to make a snap decision, especially one that involved his wife and two teenage children. So he politely responded to the president, saying he would need some time to pray and talk it over with his family.

"I'll get back to you in a few days," he said.

Lois, however, covered the extension with her hand and said to her husband, "You know we're going to go, so go ahead and tell him! You don't have to pray about it!"

And they did.

After a family council where they talked the opportunity over, they all agreed that they would like to go. The Van Cleaves spent several years in a missionary outreach to Puerto Rico.

Many years later, when the Van Cleaves were in their eighties, Marilee and I sat in a restaurant with this dear couple and asked them, "Of all the many assignments you had in the ministry, what was your favorite? What did you enjoy the most?"

Lois spoke up immediately. "Being missionaries!" she said.

True to form, Dr. Van Cleave spoke after deliberating for at least thirty seconds. "Yes," he said, "being missionaries was our favorite assignment. We could have stayed on the field all our lives. It was pure joy."

LOIS GETS THE DESIRE OF HER HEART

By the time she was middle-aged, Lois Van Cleave had lost all her relatives except for her immediate family. The Standlee family had meant the world to her as she was growing up. The family gave her the foundation of her Christian life and values. But the older family members had died, and she had lost touch with the younger generation. She longed inordinately to find any distant relative with whom she could relate. So as she and Dr. Van Cleave would travel around the country, she would look in phone books to see if there might be a Standlee. Because of the unusual spelling, they would be easy to locate, she surmised. In Miami, Baltimore, Atlanta, Chicago, Little Rock, etc., she looked, always drawing a blank.

On this day her Bible reading covered Psalm 37, including the familiar verse, "Delight yourself in the LORD and he will give you the desires of your heart" (v. 4). She claimed the verse and prayed, "Lord, You know that a great desire of mine would be to find a family member. You know I delight in You, so would You fulfill that desire, selfish though it seems?"

A few Sunday mornings later she came into our sanctuary several minutes before the service. She sat down while Dr. Van Cleave was talking to friends and started casually to peruse the church bulletin. She noticed an account of the baptismal service the previous Sunday night. There was a list of the 38 people who had been baptized. She read down the list to see if there was anyone she would know. She could hardly believe her eyes when she came across the name of a Bradley Standlee. She was so ecstatic that when her husband came to sit down she told him what she discovered. She wanted to go out and ask one of the pastors if he knew Bradley Standlee, but the studied Dr. Van Cleave told her to wait and call the church office the next day.

Later she told me that she was so excited that she didn't hear a word of what I had preached. She compromised with her husband by not leaving the service, but as soon as the service was over she darted toward Joe and asked if he knew Bradley. Of course, he knew him well. They tried to find him, but he had already gone out to eat. However, Joe called Lois that night and gave her Bradley's phone number. She said she couldn't sleep that night, and the next morning she called Bradley with bated breath. Could this be true?

Bradley answered, and after a few minutes they made the connection that they were cousins who had not seen each other since they were twelve-year-old kids, way back in Missouri. Bradley was now seventy-six, and just one month ago he had a life-changing conversion. Lois and Bradley had ten wonderful years of joyful, kindred relationship before she passed away. This seems to show us the things that are important to us are a big deal to God as well.

CHAPTER 42

THE GREATEST MIRACLE: THE TRANSFORMATION OF A LIFE

Every day there are millions of people who are making decisions to put their trust in God and follow Christ as their Savior. The following story is an example of what the Lord can do in a person's life, making him or her a new person.

JOHN CRAIG LAY IN St. Francis hospital in a comatose state and was not expected to survive.

One of our pastors, Dr. John Holmes, went to visit John Craig. Dr. Holmes talked to him for a few moments, and though Craig could not respond, he sensed that Craig was comprehending. Dr. Holmes decided that because Craig was so critical and may not survive he should pray for him to prepare him for death. He told Craig he would pray with him to receive Christ into his life and suggested that Craig would pray with him inwardly.

Dr. Holmes told Craig, "If you understand what you prayed to receive Christ as Savior and confessed that you believe Christ will give you eternal life, just squeeze my hand." Though the squeeze was ever so slight, it was certain, and Craig was able to evoke a faint smile. Later Craig told others that he knew that moment was a turning point in his life.

Within a short time Craig had recovered sufficiently to come to church. I remember that Dr. Holmes brought Craig for me to meet him. He had a huge smile on his face, was soft spoken and polite, and when I reached to shake his hand he said, "No, I want a hug." From then on at our church, Craig would always greet people, "I want a hug." He was so gregarious and Christlike that I assumed he had been a long-time Christian. But Dr. Holmes reminded me that this was the man recently saved in the hospital.

Thereon, John Craig was a mainstay of our congregation. He attended every church service and prayer meeting. It was easy to see him growing in great spiritual strides almost by the week. It seemed he had a baptism of love, loving God and people. He couldn't get enough of being with people. When he knew Christian people were getting together for any reason, he made it a point to be there. He would say that he had gone all his life trying to avoid Christians, but now he had discovered them to be "the best people on Earth, and look what I've missed all my life." He had the most healthy, loving spirit.

In his honor, members of our church often improvised the Scripture verse, "Where two or three Christians gather together, John Craig will be in their midst." Playing off a base-ball term, we often attributed John the distinction of the D.H., or our Designated Hugger. He spent the first part of the service in the foyer, not as an usher but as a hugger of all the incoming worshipers.

Additionally, he was a man of surprising depth. It was as though the Holy Spirit had given him a crash course in spiritual growth. I remember telling people that I saw in John every one of what the Bible refers to as the fruit of the spirit: love, joy, peace, patience, kindness, goodness, faithfulness, gentleness, and self-control. (See Galatians 5:22–23.)

We were all saddened by his death many years later. And was I ever shocked when John's two sons came to my study to help me prepare for John's eulogy and funeral message. "Tell me about your dad," I asked, "because I want to put together a story of his life." I kept coaxing them for things of interest from his youth. Finally, they admitted they were ashamed to talk about their dad's youth.

This was unbelievable. They proceeded to tell me their dad was a cruel, lawless ruffian. He was known as a ruthless bully. They said John grew up in the Midwest and was known to have been in a brawl in almost every saloon in Nebraska and Colorado and parts of Arizona. They told how their own youth was interrupted when law enforcement agencies came to their house looking for their father.

I was swallowing deeply, and trying to gather myself, I asked, "Are we talking about the same John?" I explained to them that was not the John we knew. "Our John," I explained, "was the nicest, most loving, gentle person you could meet. A consummate Christian."

They explained, "Dad's life turned around when he started coming to your church. We were ashamed to admit he was our father until your church changed him. It was like having a new dad, and we became very proud of him. From then on he brought us nothing but pride and happiness. He became like another person. He didn't resemble the man he used to be. We hated that man, but we loved the new man."

I protested vigorously to make it clear that the church cannot change anyone. The church's mission is to point people to Christ, who is the One who transforms people's lives. I explained the promise of the Bible that declares, "Anyone who belongs to Christ has become a new person. The old life is gone; a new life has begun!" (2 Cor. 5:17, NLT).

"That is what happened to your dad," I explained.

Because the world around us doesn't understand spiritual transformation, they often mock Christians when they use the term *born again*. That is understandable, because the religious leader Nicodemus didn't understand when Jesus said to him that one must be born again to have eternal life. (See John 3:7.)

At John's funeral, lots of people came who had been part of his old life. It was my desire they would consider accepting the new birth, which gives us:

- New preferences and lifestyle
- New priorities, a new set of desires
- New person (The old man is changed into a new man.)
- New purpose, a new reason for living

If you desire to have the new birth, pray this prayer:

> *Dear Lord Jesus, I recognize my sinful condition, and I repent for my old life. I now put my faith in You and trust in You as my Savior. I believe You are the Son of God, and I receive You into my life. Amen.*

CONCLUSION

A NATURE WRITER SPENT THREE weeks at a resort on the eastern shore of Lake Michigan. A lover of nature, it was his life's habit to be outdoors every summer evening to absorb the sunsets.

While staying at the resort, however, his passion cost him a leisurely dinner. Because of the timing of the evening meal, he would usually eat quickly, then excuse himself to go the veranda in order to watch the sunset over the lake. After a couple nights of this, a few other guests wondered what he was seeing. They also left meals unfinished in order to see what he was viewing on the deck outside. Watching the sunset together, they listened appreciatively as he called attention to subtle features of the sunset over the water.

The next night he went out again. People who had gone out with him the first night had told their friends, so this night there were twice the number on the veranda. Again, the writer quietly explained the natural phenomenon of the setting sun with its colors, shades, and beauty.

The next night more people still attended the informal sunset talk. In a couple more days, the guests requested that the managers of the resort reschedule dinner in order to follow the sunsets. By that time, everyone but the indifferent had crowded out on the veranda, enthralled by the sun's dying rays, the way the light glistened off the water, and the magnificent clouds that caught and held the light, even after the sun had slipped below the horizon. After three weeks together at the resort, everyone had come to love the sunsets. As the nature writer was packing his car to leave, one of the employees came running to thank him.

"I've been working at this resort for fifteen years," he said, "and I never saw a sunset until you came."

This story describes my heart's desire for this book. God never stops working in the lives of His kids, intervening time after time in a thousand different ways, seen and unseen.

In reality, the miracles never stop. But most of the time, we're too busy eating dinner, and we don't see them.

In the pages of this book, I have attempted to call attention to the multiple ways God works at all times in all aspects of our lives. It's my prayer that this will help those who have walked through the days of their lives and "never saw a sunset."

It's time to step out on the veranda and celebrate His glory.